Better Homes and Gardens

scrapbooking for baby

WILEY

John Wiley & Sons, Inc.

For general information about our other products and services, please contact our Customer Care Department within the United States at (800) 762-2974, outside the United States at (317) 572-3993 or fax (317) 572-4002.

Wiley also publishes its books in a variety of electronic formats. Some content that appears in print may not be available in electronic books. For more information about Wiley products, visit our web site at www.wiley.com.

ISBN 978-0-470-54802-8

Printed in the United States of America

10 9 8 7 6 5 4 3 2 1

SOMETHING ABOUT BABIES sparks a desire to scrapbook. Maybe it's because in that first year, each delightful change seems to happen so quickly that the need to preserve the moment becomes more urgent.

That happened to me with the birth of my first niece, Madison. I took so many pictures that my brother still complains about the paparazzi treatment he endured at the hospital. When I got those precious pictures back from the photo lab, it just wasn't enough to put them in a regular photo album. I felt compelled to share the story of her birth and how much that one little person—the first of a new generation—changed the whole family. In scrapbooking, I found a way to express those thoughts while showing off the photos.

In fact, I'm still scrapbooking baby photos of Madison and her sister, Avery, proving it's never too late to scrapbook baby photos. They were 5 and 2 when I finally got around to creating this page about their resemblance to each other as infants.

In the spirit of helping scrapbookers of all levels and styles fulfill the need to share the stories of the babies in their lives, we've created this special book. For new scrapbookers drawn to the hobby by the arrival of a baby, we've included a guide to getting started. For longtime scrapbookers looking for fresh designs, we've picked a variety of pages with innovative ideas for scrapping everything from pregnancy to Baby's first birthday.

Because so many of us are always minding our budgets and our schedules, we've sprinkled time-saving tips from scrapbooking moms throughout each chapter. And look for our helpful icons identifying quick and budget-friendly designs.

If that's not enough to get you started on those baby pages, there are over 100 babies in this book (some of whom show up several times) to inspire you, and I can honestly say they are all adorable. Reading just one chapter of this book is enough to catch baby fever. So consider yourself warned, and enjoy!

> When I got those precious pictures back from the photo lab, it just wasn't enough to put them in a regular photo album.

Resemblance @ 7 Months

When Avery was first born, the resemblance between her and Madison was amazing. Sometimes it is hard to tell their baby pictures apart, such as in these photos of them both at 7 months. When they were babies, you could see brief glimpses of Macenzie, Jeremy, Mom, and other family members in their little faces. I look forward to seeing whose personality traits come out as they grow up and become very different people who look very much alike.

Michelle

Michelle Rubin
Editor, *Scrapbooks etc.*

SOURCES Patterned paper: Reminisce Papers. Fonts: Airplane (title) by Two Peas in a Bucket, Euroference (journaling) off the Internet. Stickers: Autumn Leaves. Circle cutter: Fiskars. Corner rounder, circle punch: EK Success. Design: Michelle Rubin.

contents

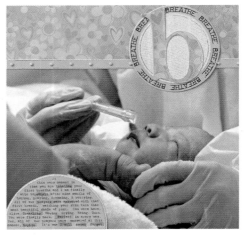

Departments

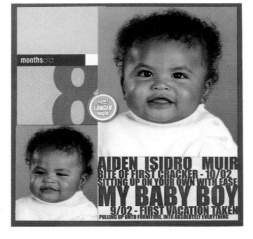

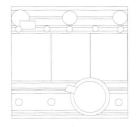

SEE THE SKETCH
The basic structure of any scrapbook page can be broken down into a sketch that you can use to envision your own design. Throughout the book, we've included sketches wherever we thought they might help you get past the layers to the bones of the page. And, as you read *Scrapbooking for Baby* and become more familiar with this handy tool, we hope you'll be able to see the sketch in your mind for any layout you come across.

$ BUDGET FRIENDLY
We know your dollars are hard earned and you want to make the most of your scrapbooking budget. Any of the designs accompanied by this icon can be reproduced for $5 or less.

MADE IN MINUTES
This book is full of quick but stylish layouts, so look for this icon on pages that can be completed in 30 minutes or less.

Get started

IF YOU'RE A FIRST-TIME scrapbooker with the urge to preserve the story of Baby's first year, here's a handy tutorial that can help you turn the pages in this book into ones that celebrate your own little one.

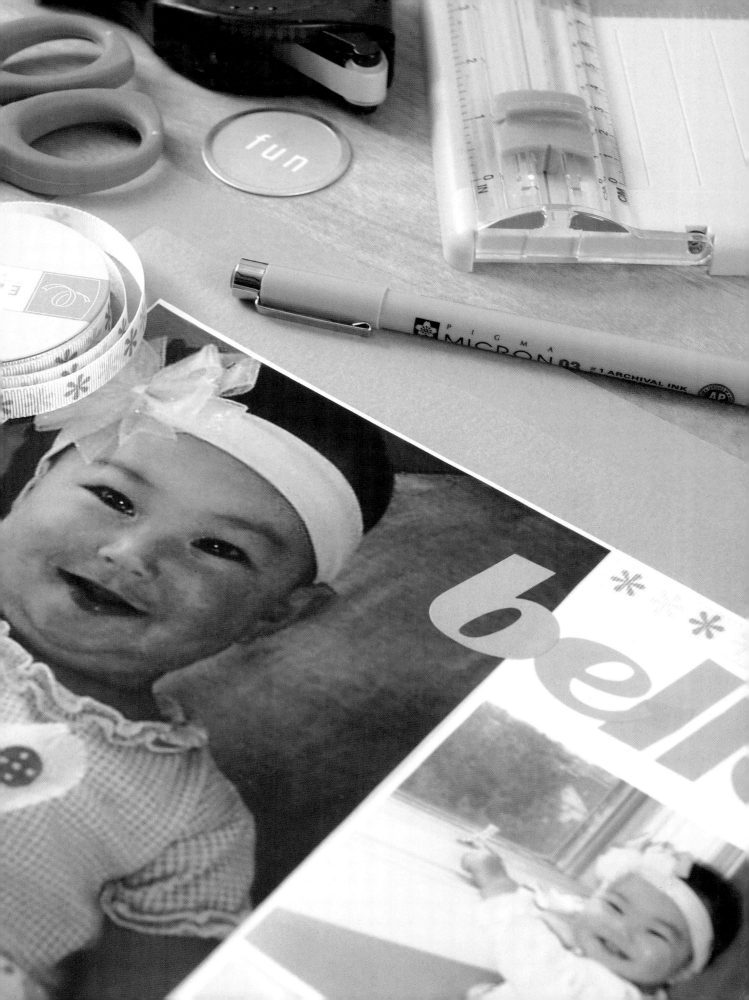

EVERY SCRAPBOOK PAGE DIFFERS, but most have the same core ingredients. Take a minute to study the anatomy of a scrapbook page, and see what yours should— or shouldn't—have.

PATTERNED PAPER: Though not a requirement, patterned paper provides pizzazz.

PHOTOS: The part of your layout that catches the eye first is usually the focal-point photo. Supporting shots are the additional photos that visually help tell your story.

BACKGROUND: Whether a solid piece of cardstock or a patchwork of patterned papers, the background frames all the elements of your page.

It's amazing to look at Brecken and see the faces of two people I love. He is the perfect reflection of Gabby and Jason and a beautiful reminder of their true

love

Brecken Hunter
July 2005

JOURNALING: As simple as a place and date or as detailed as your intimate thoughts and feelings, journaling is an important part of any scrapbook page.

EMBELLISHMENTS: Tags, ribbons, die cuts, and more add finesse to your design. You can choose to embellish a little, a lot, or not at all.

TITLE: Large and bold or small and subtle, a title introduces the subject and sets the tone.

putting it all together

NOW THAT YOU'VE GOT THE RIGHT ELEMENTS, how do you put together an actual page? We asked first-time scrapbooker and new mom Amy Spaulding to help us show you the process step-by-step.

Amy began by looking for inspiration from layouts made by other scrapbookers. She liked the look of this page by Erin Roe and thought it would work well for some cute photos of her daughter, Bella.

SOURCES Cardstock: Bazzill Basics Paper. Font: Franklin Gothic. Chipboard letters: Making Memories. Texture plates: Fiskars. Punches: EK Success. Design: Erin Roe.

In about half an hour (not including photo printing or shopping time), Amy created this adorable page that will preserve memories of her daughter for a lifetime. Check out the next two pages to see how Amy assembled the layout. Then use the lessons to turn any page you see in this book into your own custom creation.

SOURCES Stickers, ribbon, tags: American Crafts.

1 Assess your needs.

Amy saw that Erin's page required one 5×7" and two small square photos, three layers of cardstock, materials to make her title, and circle accents. She also needed a paper trimmer, adhesive, scissors, a fine-tip pen, and a circle punch.

5 MINUTES

2 Gather your materials.

She printed her photos to size before selecting the other materials. Since her daughter was wearing pink in the photos, Amy chose pink cardstock for her background and then brought in lavender and white. She found cute metal-rim tags to serve as the circle embellishments, a sheet of stickers to create her title, and a fun ribbon that brought all her colors together.

TIME VARIES

3 Crop and mat your photos.

Cropping photos (cutting away the excess image around your subject) can get rid of distracting elements or make your photo the right size. Matting photos (mounting them on slightly larger pieces of cardstock to create a frame) helps them stand out on your page. Following Erin's layout, Amy matted all her photos on one large piece of cardstock.

5 MINUTES

TIP: To get a thin, even mat on a single photo, cut a piece of cardstock ¼" longer and wider than your photo and attach your print in the center.

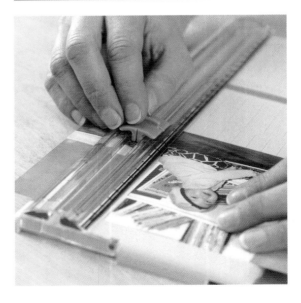

4 Attach your main elements.

Amy cut a square of lavender cardstock slightly larger than the white photo mat and punched circles as shown in the original design. She attached the white cardstock to the purple, then glued the layers to the full sheet of pink cardstock.

5 MINUTES

TIP: Get the most bang for your buck by using less. A small line of adhesive in two opposing corners and a long line connecting the other two corners will keep things in place.

5 Write your story.

Amy wrote her journaling with a fine-tip pen on a separate piece of cardstock for easy substitution in case of errors. She composed a draft and then, using a ruler and a pencil, drew lines to guide her finished copy. She checked the spacing and spelling, erased the lines, and adhered the journaling block to her page.

10 MINUTES

TIP: It's the story you choose to share that really sets a scrapbook apart from a photo album. Whether you detail events happening in the photos or express your feelings, make sure to take a few minutes to compose some journaling.

6 Add finishing touches.

For her title, Amy used large stickers to spell out "bella." She overlapped them on her photo so the whole name would fit, and she used a bit of adhesive to tack down a strip of ribbon where Erin's design had felt squares. Finally, she slipped metal-rim tags into the negative space of the punched circles to complete the look.

10 MINUTES

TIP: Embellishments help make your page even more engaging. They range from simple letter stickers to elaborate accents made of plastic, metal, and chipboard.

DESPITE ALL THE TOOLS ON THE MARKET, you really need only a few basics to get you started. As you grow as a scrapbooker and fall more in love with the process, you may want to add to your stash. For now, here are a few items every scrapbooker should have on hand.

PEN: An acid-free, black, medium-tip pen will come in handy for fast journaling or adding hand-drawn details to your pages. (See more about writing tools on page 14.)

ADHESIVE: Pick an all-purpose adhesive to start. We'd recommend starting with a tape runner. (See more about adhesives on page 16.)

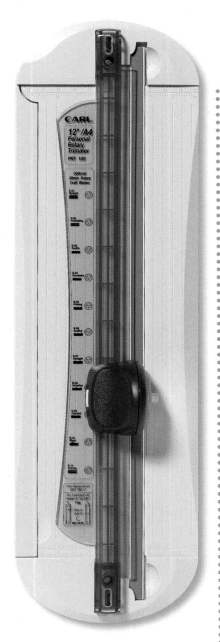

PRECISION-TIP SCISSORS: You'll reach for a quality pair of small scissors again and again. They're great for making smooth, detailed cuts. (See more about cutting tools on page 18.)

RULER: Metal is durable, but an acrylic ruler lets you see through to your project as you're measuring and placing things. Find one with a metal edge in case you decide to break out a craft knife at some point.

PAPER TRIMMER: Whether cutting cardstock or cropping photos, a 12" paper trimmer makes quick work of long straight cuts.

papers

NEXT TO YOUR PHOTOS, paper is the most important ingredient in the recipe for a great scrapbook page. Almost all scrapbooking paper sold online or in stores will be acid-free, but if you're not sure, ask. If there's no guarantee, steer clear. Acid can damage photos over time.

CARDSTOCK: If you never read beyond this paragraph, you'll be fine. Plenty of scrapbookers survive—and thrive—on a diet of pure cardstock. This multipurpose, sturdy paper is available with a smooth or textured finish and is used for backgrounds, die cuts, punched shapes, photo mats, and cards. Whether you buy cardstock by the sheet or in packs, you'll want to keep a nice mix of colors on hand.

PATTERNED PAPER: You can find scrapbook-safe patterned paper in numerous colors, textures, and designs. Take baby steps at first and buy a few sheets with subdued patterns. Unless you're working on an album where the design is repeated several times, a sheet or two of any pattern is all you'll need. A pad of coordinated patterned paper is also a good pick for a beginner. Caution: Collecting patterned paper is highly addictive!

SPECIALTY PAPERS: When you want to kick up the wow factor, reach for a specialty paper. This group includes opaque vellum; totally see-through printed or plain transparencies; velvet, flocked, and glittered finishes as well as handmade and embossed varieties. A single sheet can add texture, depth, and pizzazz to a page. You can expect to pay a higher price for these pretties, and they may require special adhesive, so plan your budget accordingly.

pens and pencils

JUST THE TICKET FOR JOURNALING, DOODLING, AND DECORATING scrapbook pages, pens and pencils are hardworking tools. Even though you'll feel like a kid in a candy store when shopping for them, resist the urge to buy pricey full sets until you've found the type you like. Choose tools that are acid-free, fade-resistant, and waterproof. Here's a breakdown of the most popular ones for scrapbookers.

FELT-TIP MARKERS: Not only do you have a choice of tip styles (monoline, chisel-point, brush, and scroll-point), but you also can buy pens that sport different tips on each end. But choosing a tip will be easier than settling on a color. Start with a few neutrals, and then add more as you need them.

GEL PENS: Chances are you've already got a couple of these at home. Their rich, sometimes iridescent or glittery, opaque colors add flair to journaling (especially on darker paper) and really make lettering and embellishments pop. Some scrappers consider a white gel pen mandatory.

COLORED PENCILS: A good pick for shading and adding highlights to letters and embellishments, they're also cool for adding color to stamped images. A blender pen, found at an art-supplies store, can smooth and soften pencil lines.

SLICK-SURFACE PENS: Just like it sounds, these markers are designed to write on slippery surfaces such as on the fronts or backs of photos, vellum, transparencies, or CDs. They're also available in a rainbow of colors, but a good black or white one will get you started.

Today's tech-savvy scrapbookers often opt for the ease of computer-made text and titles created in word-processing programs. If you're handy with a keyboard, using your computer to generate journaling is certainly an OK option. And the now widely available ink-jet models make printing out text easy and affordable. For more information on using your computer as a scrapbooking tool, see pages 184–186.

page sizes

DECIDING WHAT SIZE YOU'D LIKE your albums to be is up to you, and you don't need to feel trapped once you've made a page in one size. Try all the sizes to find out which you enjoy most. If you buy a 12×12" post-bound or three-ring album, you'll have room to house pages of any size. Below you'll see how 4×6" photos fit on three popular page sizes.

12×12": This big square is the largest standard scrapbook size and gives you room to display multiple photos on each page, add embellishments, and be creative. Cardstock, patterned paper, and specialty paper are widely available in this size since it's the preferred dimension for manufacturers.

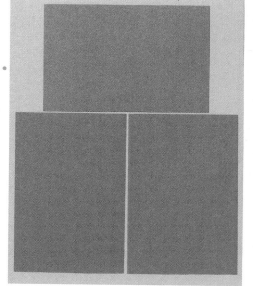

8½×11": Printing titles, journaling, and other text or clip art is easiest on 8½×11" pages. Cardstock and specialty paper (such as vellum) are often available in this size, but you also can easily cut down larger sheets.

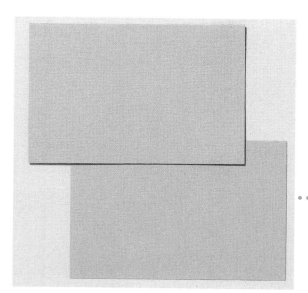

9×9", 8×8", AND 6×6": The smallest available page sizes you'll find, all three are perfect for gift of single-theme albums. 8×8" and 6×6" albums are widely available. 9×9" albums require a bit more searching but are better at accommodating 4×6" photos.

THERE ARE LOTS OF DIFFERENT TYPES OF ADHESIVES that can be used for scrapbooking. You definitely don't need to run out and buy every type right now, but it's good to know the best kind for each application. Some adhesives have a temporary bond that lets you move things around, while others become permanent over time or start out with a strong sticky factor. This guide will help you figure out which one's right for your project.

TAPE RUNNERS: Continuous rolls of double-sided adhesive are a non-messy way to mount the flat parts of a page, like photos and paper. Just drag a cartridge filled with dots, rectangles, or nonstop strips of sticky stuff along your paper or photo. Some cartridges are one-time-use, while others are refillable.
Temporary or permanent bond

SPRAYS: Sold in cans like spray paint, spray adhesives are best for quickly and evenly covering large areas. A couple drawbacks: You'll need a well-ventilated area to spray in, and if you don't cover up properly, you could wind up with sticky residue on your work surface.
Temporary or permanent bond

LIQUID GLUES: Bottles, tubes, or pens of liquid glue let you dispense any amount down to a tiny drop, which means it's a good choice for adhering delicate things like fibers, intricate die cuts, or tiny embellishments.
Permanent bond

TABS: Double-sided adhesive squares can either be dispensed from a roll in evenly spaced rows or added one by one to photos, paper, and other flat accents.
Permanent bond

GLUE STICKS: While some children's glue sticks are acid-free, check the label to make sure you're using one that's photo-safe. Glue sticks are perfect for attaching ribbon, die cuts, or other flat items to your layout.
Permanent bond

PHOTO CORNERS: Guaranteed to give you the most flexibility for adding photos to or taking them out of your scrapbook, corners are the safest option for one-of-a-kind shots. Since the photos actually slip into the corners and don't touch adhesive, they're a smart option for irreplaceable heritage prints.
Permanent bond

ADHESIVE DOTS: Superwoman-like strength makes sticky dots the go-to adhesive for bulkier objects such as buttons and beads. You'll find the dots in a variety of sizes from mini to 3-D.
Permanent bond

ADHESIVE FOAM: When you're looking for a little dimension on your page, reach for foam tape, dots, or squares. They actually lift photos and embellishments off the page for a dimensional, shadowed effect. Try this with photos, die cuts, and journaling blocks.
Permanent bond

SHEET ADHESIVES: Found in sheets or rolls, this sticky stuff offers a strong, smooth bond on flat surfaces when you need greater coverage. It can be applied by hand or with a machine like the Xyron.
Temporary or permanent bond

ADHESIVE REMOVER: Let's face it, sometimes you want to unstick what you stuck, and a photo-safe adhesive remover will do the trick. A few drops neutralize the adhesive, making it possible to cleanly lift off stickers or other things adhered to your page. You also can use a pick-up square to get rid of residual glue around the edges of items. Most art stores carry these tools.

Reach for a temporary adhesive when you want to be able to move things around. Then switch to a permanent glue when you're sure of the position.

WHAT YOU CUT WITH DEPENDS ON what you're cutting and where. One tool rarely works for every situation. Here's a rundown of the key types. Start by figuring out what you want to do and then match your cutting tool to your need.

STRAIGHT-EDGE SCISSORS: A pair of 5" microtip scissors is a must-have for your toolbox and can quickly make detailed cuts through paper, photos, vellum, and more. An 8" multipurpose pair is a handy choice for larger cuts or when cutting slightly thicker materials such as cork or thin metal.

rotary-blade

guillotine

PAPER TRIMMERS: A paper trimmer can't be beat for making long, straight cuts on paper and photos. Though they come in many sizes, a 12" trimmer, equipped with a swing-arm ruler, accommodates a variety of paper sizes and is functional at home or on the go. Three blade types to consider:
• **Sliding-blade:** To make a cut, just slide your paper in and then pull the small, replaceable blade down the length of the trimmer. The regular blade is interchangeable with a scoring one.

• **Rotary-blade:** With this type, a round, rotating blade cuts your paper. One benefit of this kind is that you can swap out the cutting blade with other blades to give your paper a fancy edge, maybe scalloped or deckled.
• **Guillotine:** Smaller, sleeker versions of the cutter you probably used in school, this tool has an arm that lifts up so you can slide in your paper. Then you lower the arm to make the cut.

CUTTING MAT: You'll need a cutting mat when working with a craft knife or shape cutter. You can choose one made of glass or self-healing rubber, and they come in many sizes. Most also have a grid that can help with measurements.

CRAFT KNIFE: A sharp craft knife has the edge over microtip scissors when you need the most control for detailed tasks such as hand-cutting titles or embellishments. It also can make long cuts like a paper trimmer, but it's not as fast, and you'll need a straightedge ruler and a cutting mat as well.

DECORATIVE SCISSORS: Available in a plentiful variety of edges (scalloped, postage-stamp, deckle, wave, etc.), these scissors are terrific for creating borders or adding a funky touch to photo edges. It's easy to get hooked on these fun tools.

RULER: Although 12" plastic or wood varieties work fine for taking measurements, metal is sturdier and acrylic has the added bonus of allowing you to see your project as you work, making cutting photo mats a cinch. Larger sizes like the 3×12" or 6×12" ones used for quilting give you more control, anchoring your paper as you work.

SHAPE CUTTERS: Adjustable tools make it easy to cut circles or ovals out of photos or cardstock.

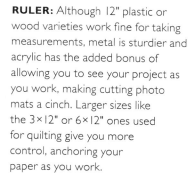

albums

ANY ALBUM YOU BUY to store your photos and scrapbook pages should be archival and acid- and lignin-free to protect and preserve your memories. To decide what type of album to get, think about what best fits your project. You may choose one kind for a scrapbook about your son's school years and a different type for an album you're giving to a friend.

THREE-RING (AKA D-RING) BINDER: Built like the notebooks you used in school, the three-ring binders for scrapbooking are archival and come in a rainbow of colors. Rings that snap apart make inserting and shuffling your pages an open-and-shut case. One pitfall? The prominent large rings tend to keep your two-page spreads a little farther apart than in other albums.

SPIRAL-BOUND: Many of these wire- or plastic-bound albums have permanently attached pages, which means they're best used for a one-topic or theme scrapbook you won't add to later. However, a new batch gives you the ability to add and remove pages. Protective page slipcovers are available for some, and this type of album is usually cheaper than others.

STRAP-HINGE: These books contain a nylon strap that threads through staples on the reinforced edges of cardstock pages. On the plus side, they're expandable, lie very flat when open, and keep two-page spreads close together. On the down side, you have to take the album apart to add or rearrange pages.

POST-BOUND: With pages bound by a set of threaded bolts that stay hidden under a flap, rearranging or adding pages means unscrewing the posts and removing the exterior pages first. Once the posts are unscrewed, adding extensions to expand the album is a cinch. Available in a wide variety of colors, sizes, and styles, this type of album can't be beat for the quantity of pages it can hold.

SNAP-LOAD: Relatively new on the market, this type of binding is very expandable and sturdy. Currently only one company makes albums that come with this binding, but you can buy a kit to retrofit post-bound albums.

Clear plastic page protectors keep your scrapbook pages dust- and fingerprint-free, extending the life of your layouts. As you shop, keep in mind the three no-nos: no acid, no lignin, no polyvinyl chloride (PVC). Quality scrapbook goods will include this info on their packaging.

HERE ARE A FEW MORE TOOLS AND SUPPLIES that might pique your curiosity. Spare your wallet by taking your time investing in tools, and check with your local scrapbook store about which tools are available for your use. Many stores let customers use die-cutting machines and punches for free when they purchase paper.

CHALKS: Applied with a dauber, sponge, cotton swab, or even your finger, chalk adds a soft hint of color to stamped images, embellishments, or journaling blocks. Swiped along the outer edges, chalk defines your page all the way around.

COLOR WHEEL: When you're trying to decide which colors would look best with your photos or a particular paper, grab a color wheel and dial up your main color. Arrows will point you to several color combinations and teach you about color relationships.

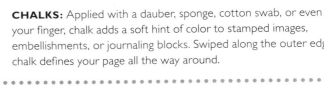
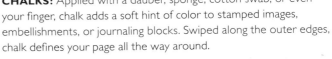

PUNCHES: Ranging in size from ½" to more than 3" and offered in a nearly endless mix of shapes, punches are an easy way to create paper embellishments. Handled punches look much like the old-fashioned paper punch, but they now punch every geometric shape. Sets of nesting punches let you layer the same shape in a variety of sizes.

DIE-CUTTING TOOLS/DIES: Like a punch, die-cutting tools cut shapes and letters from a variety of materials, but dies allow you to get bigger sizes and more intricate designs. Personal tabletop and handheld versions are great at home or at a crop. Use them to cut your titles or create custom embellishments.

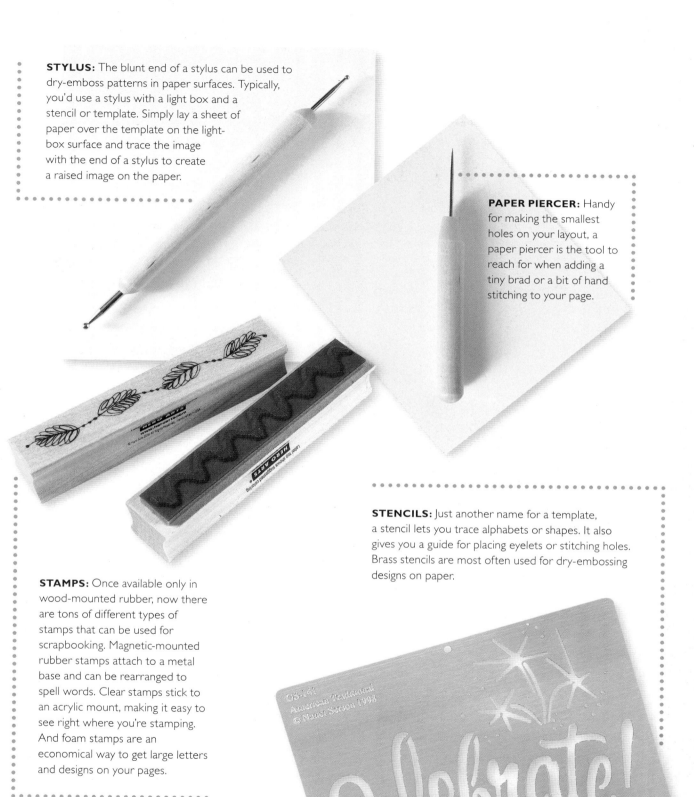

STYLUS: The blunt end of a stylus can be used to dry-emboss patterns in paper surfaces. Typically, you'd use a stylus with a light box and a stencil or template. Simply lay a sheet of paper over the template on the light-box surface and trace the image with the end of a stylus to create a raised image on the paper.

PAPER PIERCER: Handy for making the smallest holes on your layout, a paper piercer is the tool to reach for when adding a tiny brad or a bit of hand stitching to your page.

STENCILS: Just another name for a template, a stencil lets you trace alphabets or shapes. It also gives you a guide for placing eyelets or stitching holes. Brass stencils are most often used for dry-embossing designs on paper.

STAMPS: Once available only in wood-mounted rubber, now there are tons of different types of stamps that can be used for scrapbooking. Magnetic-mounted rubber stamps attach to a metal base and can be rearranged to spell words. Clear stamps stick to an acrylic mount, making it easy to see right where you're stamping. And foam stamps are an economical way to get large letters and designs on your pages.

EYELET SETTER: When paired with a hammer, a hole punch, and a craft mat, this tool mashes the back side of an eyelet, allowing you to attach tags or other bits to your page. Hammerless, spring-loaded, and squeeze-punch versions are popular.

EMBOSSING POWDER: When you want to create an embossed, or raised, image, sprinkle embossing powder (found in loads of colors and finishes) over an image stamped with slow-drying pigment ink. Use a heat tool to melt the crystals, making the image dimensional to the touch.

HEAT TOOL: Think hair dryer but not as blowy and much hotter. A heat tool is used to melt embossing powders and a few other specialty mediums.

LIGHT BOX: A light box comes in handy when you're dry-embossing paper or transferring patterns. A bulb illuminates the light box's surface from below, allowing you to see through most papers and some light-color cardstock. A bright window can serve as a substitute.

organizing supplies

WHETHER YOU'RE SCRAPBOOKING AT HOME OR AT A CROP, it's more enjoyable when your tools and supplies are organized and within easy reach. You'll work faster and be more productive if you don't have to waste time searching for your adhesive or the beautiful blue paper you know you bought.

▶ Consider investing in a multipurpose storage tote you can keep packed and ready to grab when you're on the go. They come in a range of sizes, from small briefcase models to rolling suitcase versions. Pick one that won't seem cumbersome but can grow with your passion.

▲ If you're fortunate enough to have a devoted space in which to work and store your scrapbooking stash, your storage options are nearly endless. The market is full of affordable, eye-catching storage options cleverly designed to help you organize 12×12" papers, pages in progress, tools, and more.

AS WITH ANY HOBBY, you'll need a few fundamental skills for nearly every project you attempt. In fact, many successful scrapbookers stick to these basic techniques on all their pages, never delving into the world of finishing touches you'll find beginning on page 183. And with just a little practice, you'll be able to master all of them in next to no time.

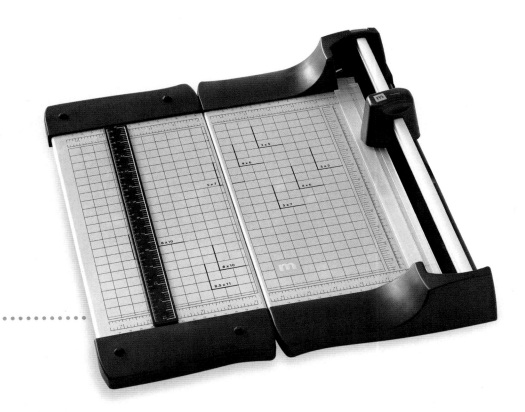

HOW DO I USE A PAPER TRIMMER? Your first few attempts to use your paper trimmer may be a little bumpy as you get used to the contraption, but before long it will be a must-have tool you'll reach for every time you scrapbook. Although there are several different trimmer styles (see page 18 for a breakdown), the most commonly used type is one with a sliding blade. Here's a quick tutorial on using one.

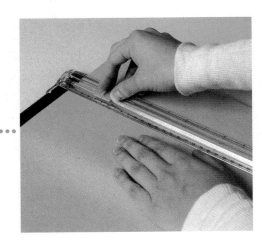

1 With the sliding blade and ruler on the right, lift up the ruler and slide your paper under it.

2 Line up the upper left corner of your paper with the measurement you want, and be sure the paper fits snugly against the upper ledge. This will ensure that your cut is straight.

3 Anchoring the paper with your left hand, lower the ruler and draw the sliding blade toward you. If you happen to be a lefty, rotate the trimmer and follow the instructions in reverse.

WHAT DOES IT MEAN TO MAT A PHOTO AND HOW DO I DO IT? Matting a photo is an easy way to make any image stand out more on your page. Usually, you'll want to choose a solid color that contrasts—but doesn't clash—with the background color of your layout. The colors in your photos will help you decide what mat to use. If in doubt, black or white is always a good default. There's not one right way to mat a photo, but here's a quick step-by-step that keeps it simple.

What you'll need: a photo • adhesive • a paper trimmer • a ruler • a piece of cardstock larger than your photo

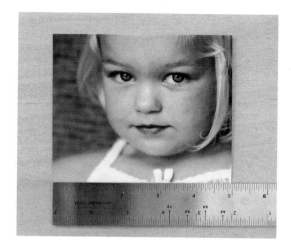

1 Measure your image vertically and horizontally.

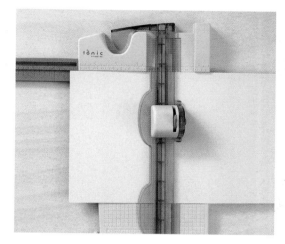

2 Cut your mat ¼" wider and longer than your photo for a ⅛" border, or vary the size depending on how much border you want around the image.

3 Add a bit of adhesive to the back of the photo, center, and adhere.

You also can attach the photo to your cardstock first and cut away the excess using your paper trimmer. Or pull out your decorative scissors for a mat with added flair!

WHY WOULD I WANT TO CROP A PHOTO AND HOW DO I DO IT? Cropping is another basic technique that every scrapbooker needs in her bag of tricks. Basically, cropping is eliminating areas of a photo that you don't need or that distract from the story you're trying to tell. Even good photos can be enhanced with smart cropping. You can crop to zero in on the action, or simply crop to make a photo fit a space on your page. Ultimately, the physical act of cropping can be done with a paper trimmer, craft knife and ruler, scissors, or even a punch. But before you start cutting, follow the simple exercise below to make sure you've identified the area you want to focus on.

You are sitting ... almost. When we prop you up and make your legs into a little tripod, you can stay upright for a few minutes. But the minute you see something you want, you reach and topple.

What you'll need: a photo • some large cardstock scraps • a paper trimmer • an acid-free pen or pencil

1 Cut two L-shape pieces of cardstock and lay them opposite each other on your photo.

2 Move them around until you're pleased with the subject, and mark the photo with an acid-free pen or pencil. Keep parts of the photo that bring context to the subject or have historical significance.

3 Use your marks to trim your photo.

Photo-editing programs make quick work of cropping digital photos. A word to the wise: always work with a copy of a print or digital file, and never crop Polaroid shots or photos that can't be duplicated.

HOW DO I HAND-CUT A TITLE? Cutting your own titles from paper and cardstock is both economical and surprisingly easy, once you get the knack of handling a craft knife. Imagine always having letters in the perfect size, color, and style for every project! Here's a simple tutorial on cutting a paper title.

What you'll need: a craft knife • a cutting mat • cardstock or paper

1 Print your title in reverse on the back of your paper or cardstock (see page 185 for step-by-step instructions on printing in reverse). If possible, use an outline version of the font to have easy lines to follow.

2 Cut out the smallest portions of your title first. Make delicate cuts, such as the center of an "e," while the word is still mostly intact to keep from ripping the paper. Rather than turning your hand or knife, gently turn the paper while you cut around curves.

3 Save the pieces you cut out to get both a positive and negative version of the word. If you don't need them for this project but the word is something you're likely to use again, save the pieces for a later project.

If you choose an uncomplicated font, you should be able to cut with precision-tip scissors rather than a craft knife. It's a great on-the-go task that can be done while riding the subway or waiting for an appointment.

BEFORE YOU TAKE YOUR FIRST STEP INTO THE SCRAPBOOKING STORE, get your photos into an order that makes sense to you. Whether you've taken the plunge into the world of digital photography or are still shooting film, it's a safe bet you've got envelopes with prints lying around. Let's tackle those first.

1 Find a spot you can claim for a few days. Set up a folding table or take over the dining room. You'll need to spread out a bit, so look for a place where your project won't be disturbed when you need to leave it. Gather all the envelopes, photos, and negatives that have been piling up.

2 Come up with categories that make sense to you. Sort photos chronologically if your goal is to complete scrapbooks by date or event. Or if you want to track on a specific life event, person, or topic, sort by themes (like vacations or birthdays). Get as specific as you want—it's your system.

3 Grab some empty boxes (plastic shoe boxes work great for this short-term storage) and line them up. Label them with your sticky notes and get ready to get organized! If you're still not sure what categories you'd like to use, dedicate a box to each family member and a few common themes such as birthdays or school photos.

4 For now, keep the negatives in chronological order in their envelopes or sleeves. We'll talk about what to do with them on the next page. Get comfy, grab your favorite snack, and start sorting your prints!

OK, I'M SORTED. NOW, WHERE SHOULD I PUT ALL THESE PRINTS? Once you've decided how to organize your photos, the next step is to find a safe place to keep them.

Archival photo boxes are widely available, fit standard-size prints perfectly, and do a bang-up job of keeping the photos safe until you're ready to use them. Create tabs for each of your topics (or dates) and you'll not only have a place to store past photos, but it'll be your first stop when sorting future prints as well.

Another great way to store prints as you're waiting to scrap them is in a **three-ring binder.** Made to accommodate all standard photo sizes, archival photo sleeves are available online or at camera and scrapbooking stores. The bonus is that you can keep a variety of photo sizes in the same place and everything's easy to see and enjoy as you flip through the book.

SHOULD I KEEP THE NEGATIVES WITH THE PHOTOS?
Actually, no. A safe place for your negatives is in PVC-free, archival polyester sleeves. The sleeves are available alone or in sheets fit for three-ring binders. The sleeves your negatives come in when you pick up pictures from the photo lab are considered a safe place for negatives as well. Since your goal is to keep them dust-free, scratch-free, and exposed to the least amount of light possible, storing negatives in a cool, dry place is a good idea, and even better if it's dark.

Your local scrapbook, crafts, or camera-supply store will offer you plenty of archival options for storage. If you can't find a place to shop locally, here are a few places online to get quality archival supplies:

www.lightimpressionsdirect.com
www.exposuresonline.com
www.kolo.com
www.archivalusa.com

DIGITAL PHOTOGRAPHY HAS SKYROCKETED in popularity, so chances are good that if you haven't already converted to digital, you're considering it. After you've invested in gear, taking photos and downloading them to a disc or hard drive costs you nothing. That means photos, or actually photo files, can easily pile up at an alarming rate. So what should you do to keep the mountain of photo files under control?

Downloading and storing files on your **hard drive**, say, by date or event, is a good storage option, but don't forget to back up those files to CDs or DVDs regularly. Getting into the habit of backing up could save you the nightmare of losing photos if your computer crashes. Photo-organization software takes storage to the next level, letting you easily browse for photos and organize them any way you like.

Not just good for backing up, **CDs** can work as your main system for storing photos, too. A CD burner is required for this option, but the discs give you quick access to photos, ensure peace of mind since they're safe if your computer goes on the fritz, and don't take up much room. If you choose this method, label the discs carefully. Better still, make index prints of the images on the CD with an image-editing program, and store the prints with the discs in albums or jewel cases. Some programs even give you the option of making customized labels for the discs.

If you want to save even more space and have a DVD burner, make **DVDs**—they hold huge amounts of photos, even a year's worth, on one disc. A rewritable DVD lets you keep adding images to it until it's full. As a backup system for smaller-capacity CDs, DVDs also fit neatly into safety-deposit boxes for long-term storage.

Storing your photos **online** is another safe option and lets you easily share your images with friends and family. As long as you keep an active account, most services will store your images indefinitely for little or nothing. Others may put a time limit on how long images can be stored or reserve the right to reduce the size of oversize images. To get the whole scoop about storage options, check out the FAQ on the site you're considering. Here are some to visit:

www.snapfish.com
www.kodakgallery.com
www.winkflash.com
www.shutterfly.com

work space

SINCE YOU'RE JUST GETTING STARTED, it may be too soon to remodel your home for a state-of-the art scrapbooking room, but it's still a good idea to think about where you'll scrap.

◀ No matter how small, a space to call your own and spread out while you're scrapbooking is ideal. You don't need a whole room; just a desk or small collapsible table will do the job nicely. If you can't find a dedicated spot, your kitchen table will work, but you probably won't be able to leave your pages in progress lying around.

▲ If your overhead lighting lacks oomph, good task lighting will help you match colors of photos and papers, and reduce the strain on your eyes while you work. To avoid shadows on your work, keep the lighting between your head and the work surface.

◀ A comfy chair that supports your lower back will boost the time you spend scrapbooking. Some scrappers prefer to stand while they're working. If that's your choice, you'll need to find a work space about the height of your kitchen counter.

Pregnancy
& preparation

BABY BOOKS CAN record what's happening even before the baby's arrival. Pregnancy is full of meaningful memories. Anticipating the baby's arrival and celebrating the pregnancy are events worthy of a special spot in your album. You also can use pre-Baby time to prepare projects that will make documenting the months to come a snap.

First Hand-Me-Down

by Candi Gershon

Candi, a mother of two, wanted to share the story of how she turned her son's room into her daughter's nursery. In journaling written like a letter to her daughter, Candi recounts the redecorating process and warm memories of moments spent in the room with both children.

TIP: Take photos of your favorite elements of your child's nursery. Then jot down any significant details, such as where the pieces came from or how you decided on the theme.

SOURCES Cardstock: Bazzill Basics Paper. Patterned paper: K&Company. Font: Miss Priss by Two Peas in a Bucket. Stickers: Me and My Big Ideas. Ribbon: Offray.

One of the benefits of having babies so close together is the sharing of the baby gear. When I was pregnant with you, we moved your brother out of the nursery and into a new "big boy room". The nursery still seemed so new to me so I didn't want to redecorate it. We decided if you were a girl we would just change out all of the blue to pink and keep the same theme. You still have to put up with the yellow walls with the blue stars, but I don't think you mind. Now that I see the room with pink accents I can't believe it was ever your brother's room. He still likes to crawl up into the crib and show you how to work the music on your aquarium he is so helpful! I love the furniture in your room so much. I bought almost everything at Pottery Barn Kids. The glider is one of my favorite places to sit with you. It is where I nursed your brother to sleep every night, and now where you are nursed to sleep too. The bookshelf holds all of your little baby books and someday you'll love to pull them out one by one and look at them. The changing table has become a catch all for blankets, jammies, bibs, and other miscellaneous baby stuff. We rarely use it for its intended purpose... changing you. The sleigh crib is where you go to sleep each night, although by the morning you are usually in our bed (you love to snuggle). So, the nursery is your very first hand me down and your very first shared memory with your brother. I hope you like it as much as he did.

fiRST HanD-me-DOWn

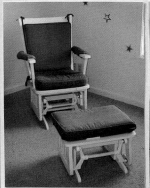

18 Weeks
by Angela Marvel

Angela played a guessing game with friends and relatives, each taking a shot at pinning down the baby's gender. Then she used their responses as casual journaling. She tucked the answer under the date flap in the lower left corner.

TIP: Turn an 8½×11" sheet on its side for a horizontal layout that gives you more room for a long title.

SOURCES Patterned paper, twill, brad: Carolee's Creations. Stickers: Mustard Moon ("18"), Doodlebug Design (letters). Chipboard letters: Pressed Petals. Pen: Sharpie. Acrylic paint: Jo Sonja's.

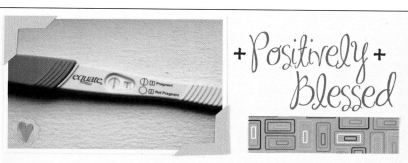

Positively Blessed
by Kristina Proffitt

As soon as Kristina read her positive pregnancy test, she sat down to write about how she was feeling. She combined her heartfelt journaling, written as a letter to her unborn child, with a photo of her pregnancy test.

TIP: Capture raw emotion by journaling "in the now," and record the thoughts and feelings you had the minute you learned the news.

SOURCES Cardstock: Bazzill Basics Paper. Patterned paper, sticker: KI Memories. Fonts: MA Sexy (title) off the Internet, Pure Imagination (journaling) by Two Peas in a Bucket. Punch: EK Success.

Waiting   by Tracy Odachowski

The placement of Tracy's title and journaling draws attention to the cute faux belly her son donned in anticipation of his baby sister's arrival.

TIP: When planning your layout, think of areas you want to emphasize, and then find ways to draw the viewer's eye to them.

 SOURCES Cardstock: Club Scrap. Patterned paper: Polar Bear Press. Rubber stamps: Stamp Craft. Ink, pen: Stampin' Up!. Acrylic letters, rub-ons: Heidi Swapp.

Big Baby Belly   by Jaclyn Rench

Using photos taken throughout her pregnancy, Jaclyn put together a layout that tracks the growth of her belly.

TIP: Take frequent pictures of your changing profile using the same pose and composition for each shot. Crop each one to the same size and line them up side by side to track your progress.

SOURCES Cardstock: Bazzill Basics Paper (green), Making Memories (blue). Font: Peachy Keen by Two Peas in a Bucket. Ribbon: Offray. Safety pins: Making Memories. Rub-ons: KI Memories (red), Autumn Leaves (white). Brad: Provo Craft. Charm: Pebbles Inc.

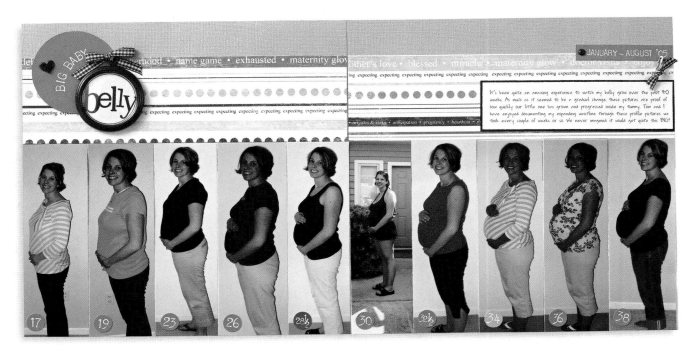

Before the baby's born, get a *head start* on your baby's album—put scrapbooking supplies on your *shopping* list along with all the baby necessities.

Helen Naylor, 2004 Creative Team member

X3 by Michelle Rubin

To celebrate the news of her friends' soon-to-arrive triplets, Michelle created a playful page using doodlelike patterned paper, rub-ons, and a cartoonish font.

TIP: Make a hidden home for ultrasound prints by raising your main photo off the page with strips of adhesive foam and tucking the ultrasound pics underneath.

SOURCES Cardstock: Bazzill Basics Paper. Patterned paper, rub-ons: Autumn Leaves. Fonts: House Brush (title) by House Industries, Century Gothic (journaling). Buttons: SEI. Chipboard accents: Heidi Swapp. Acrylic paint: Delta. Software: Adobe Photoshop Elements.

SOUND ADVICE

They're small, dark, and printed on flimsy paper, yet ultrasound pictures are an important part of your pregnancy. They deserve a home in your scrapbook. Here are a few ideas for working with these early baby pics:

• **Digitize them.** Because ultrasound photos tend to fade over time, it's best to make copies that will last. Computer scanning makes this easy. If you don't have a scanner, check with your local photo processor to see if they offer the service, or use a self-service photo kiosk.

• **Work with copies.** Whether you scan the originals or simply take your prints to a copy store, consider keeping your one-of-a-kind prints intact by scrapbooking duplicates. Remember to print copies on scrapbook-friendly paper or photo stock to make sure they'll last.

• **Get a clear picture.** Use your photo-editing software to convert the ultrasound photo to a duotone, which changes black in a black-and-white image to another color. The addition of color adds some spark. You can get a similar effect at some photo kiosks.

• **Consider captioning.** Label baby parts on the ultrasound image using your photo-editing software or a photo-safe pen. This helps others see which part is which.

• **Think small.** To keep all your ultrasound photos in one place, make a miniature album of them with tab dividers labeling each visit.

• **Group for impact.** Cluster ultrasound prints from different doctor's appointments together on one page so you can easily see the baby's growth.

• **Create enclosures.** Tuck images inside an envelope tied with ribbon and affix them to a layout if you want to include the photos but would rather not have them as the focal point of the design.

• **Focus on your feelings.** Dedicate a page in your album to recording how you felt when you saw your baby for the first time. Make the journaling the focus and include small ultrasound images as accents or on a second page.

My feet have disappeared. Now when I look down, all I see is belly. I actually have to lean over to see my feet.

And my big belly doesn't just affect my view of my feet.

I need help getting up if I'm on the floor.

I can't bend over.   Shave my legs? Ha!

Putting on socks? Yeah, not so easy.

Can't just slip behind someone in the hall, my belly tends to bump into them.

Even sitting in certain positions is uncomfortable!

Not to mention my big belly has made my innie an outie!

yoo hoofeet
...Where are you?

Give your page title punch by mixing multiple colors of the same sticker style.

Yoo Hoo Feet by Erin Sweeney

For this comical layout about a phenomenon every pregnant woman experiences, Erin wrote about the different ways her growing belly affected her day-to-day life.

TIP: Frame part of a photo to draw attention to it. Erin chose a wood frame to highlight the barely-there view of her feet from above.

SOURCES Cardstock: Bazzill Basics Paper. Patterned paper, stickers, frame: Chatterbox. Font: Bookman Old Style. Rub-ons: Imagination Project. Brads: Accent Depot from Hot off the Press.

Write stats from each doctor's visit on your calendar to use later on your pregnancy album.

Shannon Tidwell, 2005 Creative Team member

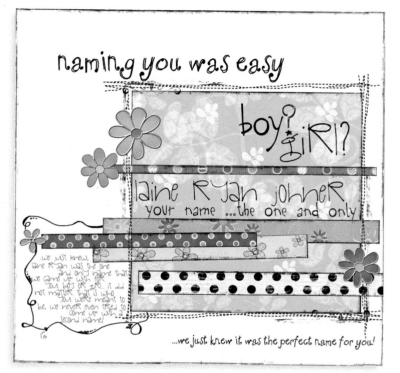

Naming You Was Easy by Jennifer Johner

Jennifer made her baby's name the center of this photo-free page, expressing her feelings about "the perfect name" through a whimsical design.

TIP: Don't wait for a photo of your baby to create a page about his or her name—tell the story by turning the journaling and title into graphic page elements that capture attention.

SOURCES Software: Adobe Photoshop. Fonts: Peanut Butter (names, journaling), Fabulous ("boy"), Secret Pal (title, subtitle) by Two Peas in a Bucket. Digital elements: Two Peas in a Bucket (papers, flowers, stitches), 8Nero (background).

Pink by Kim Haynes

Kim snapped lots of photos of the little things that make her baby girl's nursery a very special spot.

TIP: Experiment with detail shots to capture the complete story. Often, a series of close-ups says more than a single overall view ever could.

$ **SOURCES** Patterned paper: Anna Griffin. Stickers: Pebbles Inc. (flower), Scrapworks (circles, letters). Brads, paper flowers: Making Memories.

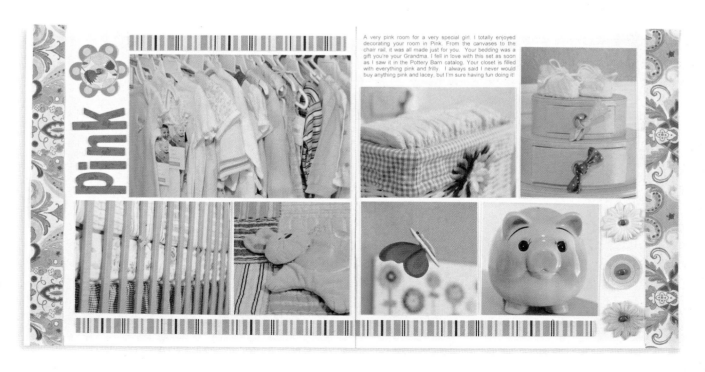

A very pink room for a very special girl. I totally enjoyed decorating your room in Pink. From the canvases to the chair rail, it was all made just for you. Your bedding was a gift you're your Grandma. I fell in love with this set as soon as I saw it in the Pottery Barn catalog. Your closet is filled with everything pink and frilly. I always said I never would buy anything pink and lacey, but I'm sure having fun doing it!

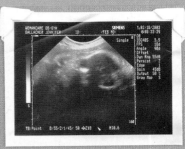

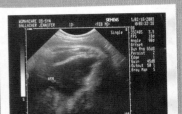

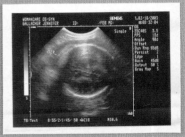

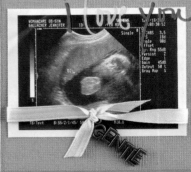

When I think about the possibilities of whom you will become,

I can hardly believe that I am the one blessed to receive you.

I only hope that I am deserving of such a precious gift.

I anticipate your arrival, my sweet little boy!

Enhance black-and-white ultrasound pictures with colorful and dimensional embellishments.

Anticipate by Jennifer Gallacher

In this layout, Jennifer showcased her ultrasound photos alongside her feelings of anticipation for her baby boy's arrival.

TIP: Treat a number of small photos as a single cohesive grouping. Jennifer contained hers with photo corners on the top image and a ribbon on the bottom one.

SOURCES Patterned paper: Déjà Views for the C-Thru Ruler Company. Font: Antique Type by Scrap Village. Ribbon: Offray. Buttons: Making Memories. Charm: Karen Foster Design. Decorative-edge scissors: Fiskars.

Oops—We Did It Again

by Brenda-Mae Teo

A tongue-in-cheek title and a tightly cropped photo work together as the focal point on this layout about Brenda-Mae's positive pregnancy test results.

TIP: Why limit your journaling to a square block? Use photo-editing or word-processing software to wrap text in special shapes that turn it into graphic elements.

$ SOURCES Cardstock: Bazzill Basics Paper. Patterned paper: Chatterbox. Fonts: Nimbus San (title) off the Internet, Century Gothic (journaling). Snaps: Making Memories.

Create an *album* before your baby comes, leaving spaces for the content you'll add later. Then all you'll have to do is drop in the *photos and journaling* as you go.

Patricia Anderson, 2006 Creative Team member
(To see an example of Patricia's idea, turn to *page 48*)

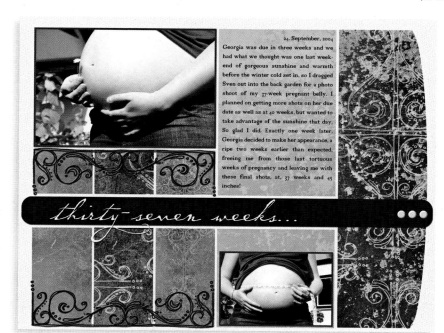

Thirty-Seven Weeks

by Amber Ries

Amber digitally designed this layout using a downloaded kit and digital brushes.

TIP: Show the scale of your growing belly by photographing it with other objects, such as a little flower and a measuring tape, as Amber did.

SOURCES Software: Adobe Photoshop CS2. Digital elements: Scrapbook Bytes. Fonts: 18th Century (journaling), Dearest Swash (title) off the Internet.

36 Weeks by Heather Melzer

Heather made her pregnant profile the clear focus of this digital page by enlarging the shot to 12" high. She documented her feelings about the birth of her second daughter with a large block of journaling.

TIP: Try posing outdoors to add a feeling of seasonality or in front of a background, such as a Christmas tree, to give context to your pregnancy photo.

SOURCES Software: Microsoft Digital Image Pro. Fonts: Mbell (journaling), Exmouth ("36," "new life") off the Internet. Digital elements: Digital Design Essentials.

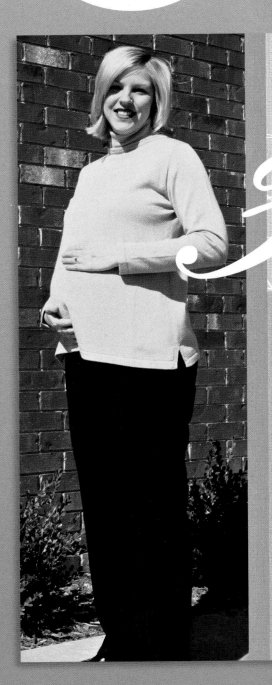

So many emotions, so much going on that it would be a shame for me not to record. Terror, excitement, stress - Tom and I are a bundle of nerves while awaiting our second child, baby Katie. I have been having contractions for the past two weeks that just seem to get more frequent and intense as the days go by. A simple trip to the grocery store has me grabbing my belly and breathing deeply every five minutes or so. Will she be late like Mackenzie was, or is she ready to come out now? Only time will tell. We have been trying to figure out what our plan of action will be for when I go into labor, but without knowing what time of day everything will happen, it forces us to play-it-by-ear. I truly am so excited to meet our little Kate, but I'm also so terrified this time around. Labor with Mackenzie was very, very hard and the pain was excrutiating. I lived through it and now we have the sweetest, most darling little girl I've ever seen. I can't even imagine having two sweet little girls in our lives, but soon we will. I just hope that labor is easier this time around. My midwifes say it will be, but I was sick for four weeks longer this time and the contractions I'm feeling now are so much more intense. Work has been very stressful for Tom and I, also. Tom's company is going through layoffs and I have more recruiting needs than I can possibly fill. I am so thankful for my work-at-home arrangement that allows me to wear comfortable clothes and eat Hostess cupcakes every couple of hours (Kate is sure to be a diehard chocaholic with as many as I've consumed in the past few months). I have to venture downtown on Friday of this week for an interview day and I'm hoping that I don't go into labor while in transit. Hopefully my visit to the doctor tomorrow morning will provide some details on how much longer it will be before she's here. Something tells me she's just as anxious to meet us as we are to meet her.

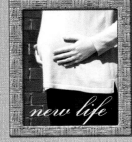

new life

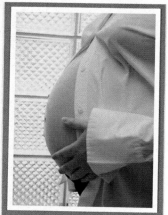

Little Caylin I have experienced so many different things since I found out that I was pregnant with you. Sure I had my share of morning sickness in the beginning and now that I am almost 6 months, I am starting to experience the lovely heartburn and lower back pain that comes along with all of these body changes, but it's all worth it. It's surreal to think about the beautiful miracle that God is creating inside of me. How did I get so lucky? How did I get so blessed in life? My absolute favorite part about being pregnant with you (so far) is my big pregnant belly! It definitely is growing each week and that is just a reminder that you are growing, too. I know I have a lot ahead of me when it comes to getting my old body back, but I'm not worried about it because pretty soon I'll have you in my arms and life as I knew it will have changed for the better. Thank you for your little kicks, which I'm sure will turn into big kicks in no time. I hope you can feel it when I rub my belly and talk to you. I can't wait to meet you, little one.

Worth the Weight by Kristina Proffitt

Kristina's play-on-words title sets the tone for this page highlighting her feelings about the physical changes she experienced in her sixth month of pregnancy.

TIP: Think outside the box when you create titles for your pregnancy layouts. Look to popular phrases, song and movie titles, and famous quotes for inspiration.

SOURCES Cardstock: Bazzill Basics Paper. Font: Acoustic Light off the Internet. Stickers: American Crafts ("worth," "weight"), KI Memories ("the"). Chipboard accent: Heidi Swapp (large heart). Punch: Impress Rubber Stamps (small hearts). Ribbon: American Crafts.

Whompus Baby by Amanda Probst

Amanda told the story of the funny nickname her sons gave her unborn baby in this easy-to-assemble layout.

TIP: Think about symmetry and balance when creating two-page designs. The right side of Amanda's layout is a flipped version of the left side, which connects the pages harmoniously.

SOURCES Cardstock: Bazzill Basics Paper. Font: Century Gothic. Stickers: American Crafts. Leather flowers, brads: Making Memories.

After our "big" ultrasound back in March, we informed the boys that they'd be getting a new baby brother. Noah, incredulously, just stared at us and remarked, "but I only thought of girl names!" It only took a few minutes, though, for him to adjust and start asking what we would name this newest baby brother. Amid his numerous suggestions (wish I'd kept a list...among the more interesting were Chartreuse and Aquamarine), he came up with Whompus and it stuck. I'm pretty sure it came from watching "Harry Potter" and seeing the Whomping Willow, which Noah referred to as the Whompus Tree...Ever since this little one keeps whomping on me from inside. After that, Noah and Asher started to have "conversations" with little Whompus. They usually went something like this:

"Hi, Whompus. This is Noah."
"You's inside Mommy."
"Daddy's sitting behind me."
"Good-bye."

Yup, short but sweet. They'd lean down to talk to him and sometimes even give him a kiss or use him as a drum or pillow. (Often, as the pregnancy progressed, their conversations consisted of telling him to stop kicking Mommy...such good, concerned boys.)

Within a couple of (long) weeks, we did finally decide on an actual name. We went ahead and spilled the beans beforehand this time around, as it would have been asking a lot of the boys to keep that secret or we'd have had to keep it from them as well. We wanted the boys to know, though, so that they could start using the name instead of Whompus. It was adorable, but I was just having a hard time picturing my three boys...Noah, Asher & Whompus.

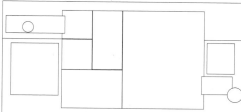

see the sketch

See how the grouping of photos on the first page balances out the large image on the second page?

Baby Shower by Jaclyn Rench

Jaclyn picked a patterned paper with a hip retro-flavor design and then built on the color scheme and circular motif to give this layout about her baby shower a playful yet sophisticated look.

TIP: Balance a page packed with photos with one that has more air for a design that's easy on the eyes. To fit in lots of shots, play with cropping and give yourself permission to use unusual sizes.

SOURCES Cardstock: Bazzill Basics Paper. Patterned paper, sticker: Autumn Leaves. Font: Cleanliness by Autumn Leaves. Dies, die-cutting tool: QuicKutz. Rubber stamps: A Muse Artstamps (walking woman), Savvy Stamps ("baby"). Ink: Marvy Uchida.

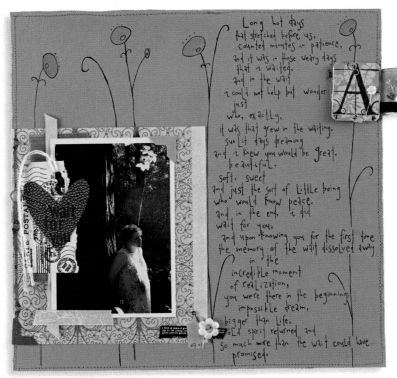

Wait for You by Ashley Calder

Ashley paired hand-drawn flowers with poetic journaling in this artistic layout that expresses how she felt while waiting for her little one to arrive.

TIP: Doodle on your layouts for cool art that doesn't cost a penny. Practice first on scrap paper, and once you get a design you like, draw it right on your page. Ashley added color to her doodling with watercolor paints.

SOURCES Decorative paper: FiberMark. Rub-ons: 7Gypsies (postage), Heidi Swapp (flower), Scrapworks (letters). Rubber stamp: MaVinci's Reliquary. Ink: Tsukineko. Pen: Sakura of America. Watercolor: Pentel. Decorative tape: Heidi Swapp (orange), 7Gypsies (text). Tags: Avery Dennison (shipping), Chatterbox (wood), K&Company (die cut). Ribbon: Wrights (wide green), American Crafts (yellow dot), The Ribbon Jar (pink velvet). Flower: Serendipity Designs. Clip: K&Company.

One Month

Two Months

Three Months

Four Months

Five Months

Six Months

Seven Months

Eight Months

Nine Months

Ten Months

Eleven Months

One Year!!!

Monthly Album Tags
by Michelle Rubin

Michelle made this set of tags as a shower gift for a pregnant friend who was worried she wouldn't have time to scrapbook after her baby arrived. Now the tags can be used to quickly label each spread in a month-by-month album.

TIP: Create matching journaling blocks and photo mats for standard-size prints when you make the tags.

SOURCES Font: Meaningful by Autumn Leaves. Stickers: Marcella by Kay for Target. Buttons: American Traditional Designs. Ink: Tsukineko.

make-ahead album

Patricia Anderson channeled her expecting-mom excitement into creative energy and started making a baby book before her son was born. All she had to do after her son's arrival—when free time was scarce—was add photos and journaling.

1. Cover the front of a purchased wire-bound album by cutting paper to size and punching holes for the wire binding along one edge. Then cut slits leading to the holes and slide the paper over the wire as you glue it in place.

2. Create a multi-use template that can be used throughout the book—in this case, journaling is on the left and photos on the right. Add embellishments, leaving corner edges loose so they can overlap photos or journaling.

3. With the majority of the work finished before the baby is born, all you have to do after the baby's arrival is size your photos, write your journaling, and plug both into the alotted spaces.

SOURCES Album: K&Company. Patterned paper: Autumn Leaves (yellow, dots), Rusty Pickle (striped, green). Fonts: Cadence by Autumn Leaves ("Delivery"), Times New Roman (journaling). Tags: Rusty Pickle (kraft), Autumn Leaves (yellow). Stickers, hardware: Rusty Pickle. Buttons, twill: Autumn Leaves. Brad, chipboard letters: Making Memories. Acrylic paint: DecoArt. Album closure: 7Gypsies. Design: Patricia Anderson.

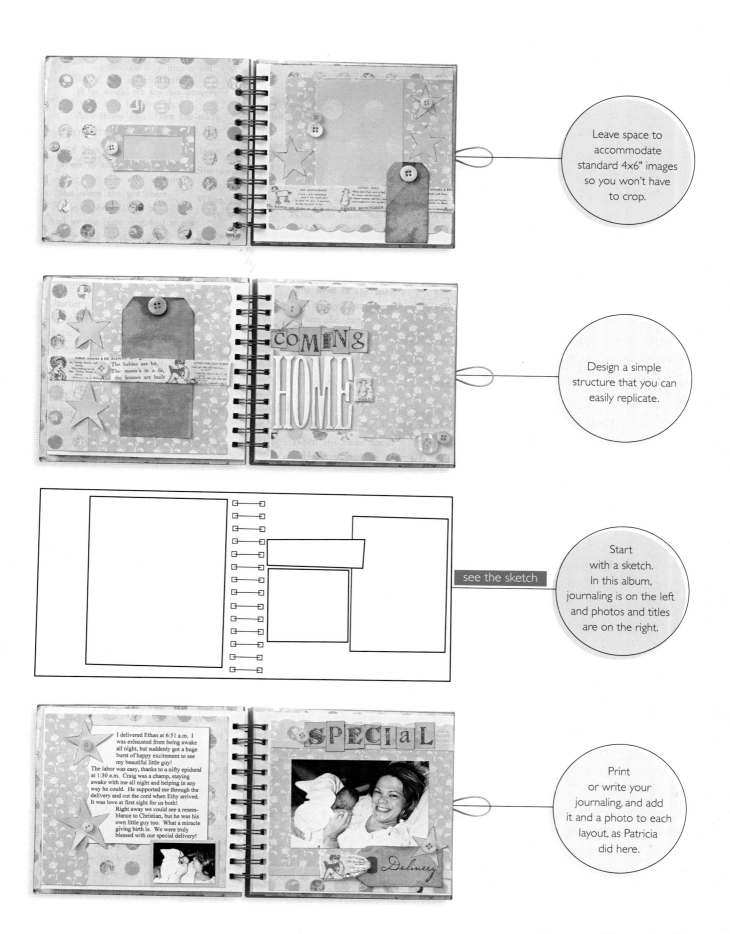

Leave space to accommodate standard 4x6" images so you won't have to crop.

Design a simple structure that you can easily replicate.

see the sketch

Start with a sketch. In this album, journaling is on the left and photos and titles are on the right.

COMING HOME

I delivered Ethan at 6:51 a.m. I was exhausted from being awake all night, but suddenly got a huge burst of happy excitement to see my beautiful little guy!

The labor was easy, thanks to a nifty epidural at 1:30 a.m. Craig was a champ, staying awake with me all night and helping in any way he could. He supported me through the delivery and cut the cord when Ethy arrived. It was love at first sight for us both!

Right away we could see a resemblance to Christian, but he was his own little guy too. What a miracle giving birth is. We were truly blessed with our special delivery!

SPECIAL

Delivery

Print or write your journaling, and add it and a photo to each layout, as Patricia did here.

Welcoming Baby

FINALLY! THE LONG-awaited day has arrived. From the baby's birth to those first exciting days at home, every memorable moment makes prime scrapbooking material. In this section, find tons of ideas for scrapbooking newborn photos, as well as ideas for making baby announcements and saving precious memorabilia.

Let your words
be heard by
printing text on a
solid background—
a busy pattern will
overpower text and
make it hard to read.

She by Heather Crawford

Working with photos with lots of color, Heather opted for a neutral palette and subdued patterns for this page about her baby boy and his very special birth mother.

TIP: Arrange photos in an L shape throughout your album to fit in lots of shots with little headache. Boost interest by rotating the design for some pages.

SOURCES Patterned paper: Scrapworks (blue), KI Memories (stripe), Anna Griffin (floral). Stickers: Scrapworks. Rub-ons: Chatterbox. Metal letters: American Crafts. Flower: Michaels.

She is Rachel, Chaz's birthmother. She lived in Omaha, us in Atlanta, and we were brought together by an agency in Washington State, although we all know that our lives intersected according to a much bigger plan. She found herself in a not so good situation—unmarried, another baby already, an unhealthy relationship and lifestyle. Rachel made the very brave, wise, and unselfish decision to choose adoption for her baby, going to great lengths to ensure her plan happened. She picked up everything and moved to another state in her last month of pregnancy to ensure that the adoption was not interrupted like she knew would be attempted. We were the lucky ones she chose to be the parents to this beautiful child and to get to experience the joy of having a baby—something we had been unable to do on our own. She even chose me to be the one person in the delivery room with her, allowing me to experience his entry into this world-- the closest I will ever come to experiencing childbirth myself. Rachel never wavered or changed her mind, even when things got messy later with Chaz's birthfather and the finalization of the adoption. For Rachel and our child, there are really no words to describe our gratitude and love. We will forever have the bond of this experience, and Chaz will always know who Miss Rachel is and what a wonderful woman she is.

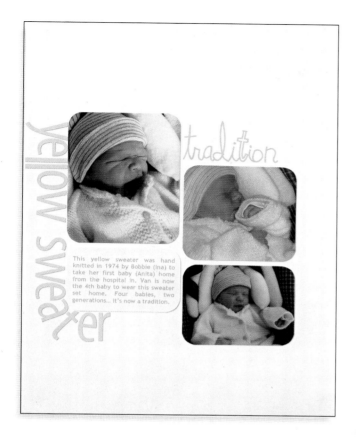

Yellow Sweater

by Jennifer Harrison

A hand-knit yellow sweater has become the official homecoming apparel for newborns in Jennifer's family.

TIP: Round corners with a punch to soften the edges on your pages. It's also a subtle nod to earlier decades—ideal for a design about family traditions.

 SOURCES Cardstock: Pebbles In My Pocket. Font: Trebuchet MS off the Internet. Stickers: Doodlebug Design. Rub-ons: KI Memories.

> Look for good page *titles* in the free magazines you get when you have a new *baby.* Magazine layouts also can *translate* into a scrapbook page.
>
> Lisa Storms, 2006 Creative Team member

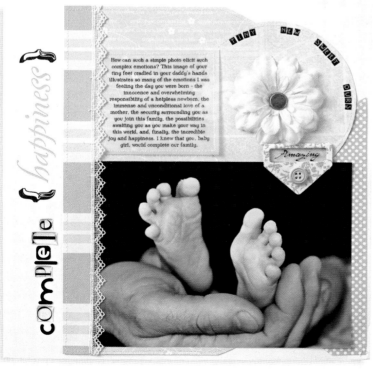

Complete Happiness

by Angelia Wigginton

A striking black-and-white photo of her husband's hands cradling their baby's tiny feet spurred Angelia to create a layout to house her thoughts about the new arrival.

TIP: Use your camera's macro setting to take close-ups of your little one's small features.

SOURCES Cardstock: Bazzill Basics Paper. Patterned paper: Sweetwater. Vellum: The Paper Company. Stickers: KI Memories. Rub-ons: K&Company ("happiness"), Autumn Leaves (brackets). Tab: Creative Imaginations. Epoxy letters: K&Company (title), Creative Imaginations (small). Button, lace: Making Memories. Brad: Karen Foster Design. Flower: Michaels.

VSD by Jackie Pettit

Jackie made sure she had lots of space to tell her serious story but softened the mood with a large powder blue heart in the background.

TIP: Record it all. Our lives aren't always picture-perfect; even scary, uncertain, and hard times deserve a place in our memories and albums.

SOURCES Cardstock: KI Memories (blue), Bazzill Basics Paper (white). Patterned paper, acrylic letters: KI Memories. Font: Century Gothic. Safety pin: EK Success.

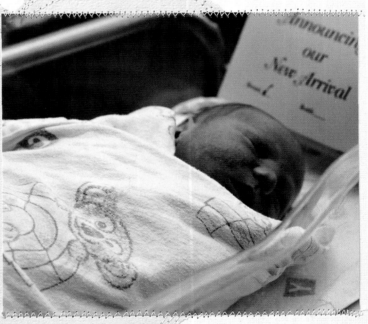

Babies fill a hole in your heart you never knew existed.

When you were 48 hours old, your nurse was doing your morning assessment and heard a heart murmur that she didn't hear before. She told our pediatrician when she came in, and she listened to you and heard it also. She said that it sounded "harsh" and unlike the typical newborn murmur. She suggested that we get an echocardiogram to check for any congenital heart defects before we took you home from the hospital. They performed the echo and we learned that you had a VSD which stands for Ventricular Septal Defect. A VSD is an opening in the wall that separates the two ventricles of the heart. Because your VSD is small, we were told that you should not have any symptoms and that you would not need to have surgery.

We also found out that you had mild tricuspid valve insufficiency, and an aortic arch anomaly. We went to see a Pediatric Cardiologist when you were 3 weeks old that confirmed this. She said that the VSD could take up to 10 years to close, but hopefully it will close by the time you are a year old. This was such a relief, because I take care of the babies who have to have their heart defects surgically repaired, and I sure didn't want my sweet little guy to have to go through that. We took you back at 6 months for a follow up visit, and learned that your VSD had closed on its own, but your PFO (Patent Foramen Ovale) is still open. Now we have to take you back again for another visit when you are 12 months old to make sure that the PFO closes.

From this moment on...

...she will protect you, *love* you, teach you. she will learn quickly how to be a big *sister* you in return will bother her, take her things & generally pester her the way little *brothers* do. years from now, the *two* of you will understand how *special* the bond between you is. I hope someday you will be *friends*, as well as siblings. you will follow her, trust her, *love* her as deeply as she already loves you. from this moment on, *forever*, it's you & her – little brother & big sister.
w b g 2.25.2004

who big sister
where hospital
when birth day

cherish

Cherish by Heather Thompson

A tender moment between new siblings inspired Heather to create this page, which includes blue and pink to reflect both children.

TIP: Use a combination of fonts, or follow Heather's lead and mix your own handwriting with computer type to single out key words or phrases.

$ SOURCES Patterned paper, sticker: SEI. Font: Baskerville Old Face off the Internet. Rub-ons: Doodlebug Design (stitches), Melissa Frances (phrase). Chipboard accent: Heidi Swapp. Pen: American Crafts.

Mommy & You by Sarah Tyler

Though vanity tempted her to skip scrapbooking these photos, Sarah realized that she wanted to celebrate the memory of snuggling with her newborn at the hospital.

TIP: Create unique photo mats by mounting your photos on nontraditional materials, such as wire mesh, chipboard, or fabric.

SOURCES Cardstock: Prism Papers. Patterned paper: Scissor Sisters. Mesh: Magic Mesh. Stickers: Pebbles Inc. Rubber stamps: Leave Memories (title), Wordsworth ("&"). Ink: Jacquard.

Send a *digital* baby announcement in the form of a cute photo with details included in the *e-mail.*

Heather Melzer, contributing editor

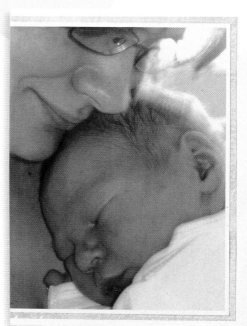

MOMMY & YOU

bringing *joy*

I got to spend lots of time snuggling you during our stay at the hospital. I was so amazed that you had come! I just kept holding & looking at you! You're such a sweet little baby. I love you!

Look for the labels "acid-free," "buffered," and "lignin-free" when shopping for supplies to make sure your precious photos stay safe and well-preserved.

Breathe by Renee Villalobos-Campa

A large, close-up photo of her daughter just moments after birth has a huge impact on Renee's page celebrating her daughter's first breaths.

TIP: Take a cue from your photo's colors. Renee makes her daughter's pink skin tone the dominant hue on the page, bringing the focus to the newborn.

SOURCES Cardstock: Provo Craft (yellow), Prism Papers (teal). Patterned paper: Provo Craft. Font: Harting (journaling), Mechanical Fun (title) off the Internet. Shape template: Provo Craft. Chipboard accent: BasicGrey. Brads: Junkitz. Pen: Staedtler.

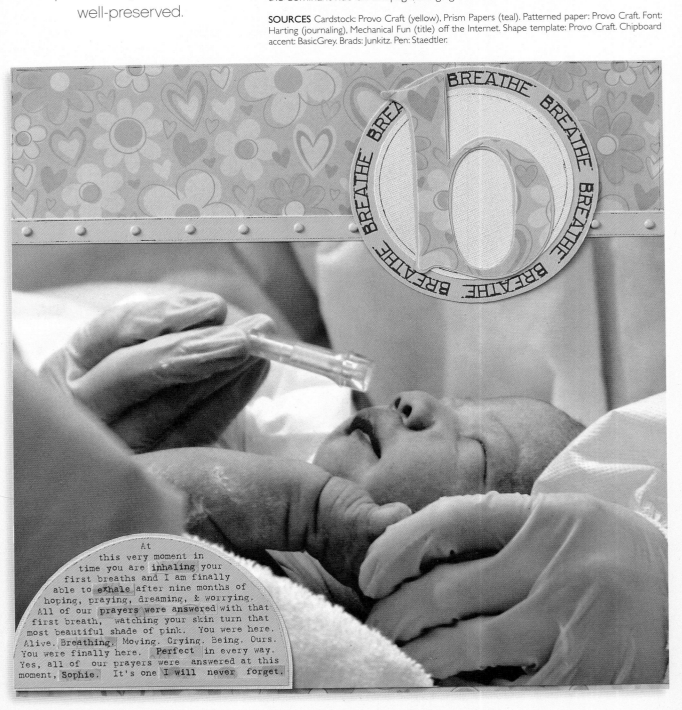

At this very moment in time you are inhaling your first breaths and I am finally able to exhale after nine months of hoping, praying, dreaming, & worrying. All of our prayers were answered with that first breath, watching your skin turn that most beautiful shade of pink. You were here. Alive. Breathing. Moving. Crying. Being. Ours. You were finally here. Perfect in every way. Yes, all of our prayers were answered at this moment, Sophie. It's one I will never forget.

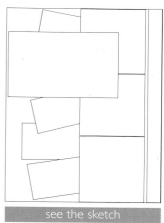

see the sketch

Love by Allison Kimball

Allison filled this page with snapshots of her with her newly adopted son and tags filled with journaling all about their first meeting.

TIP: Exaggerate a little. The oversize title Allison used on this page makes a big impression that bolsters the message.

SOURCES Patterned paper: Daisy D's Paper Co. Pen: American Crafts. Chipboard accent: Li'l Davis Designs. Ribbon: Making Memories. Tags: 7Gypsies (ivory), Li'l Davis Designs (stitched), Pebbles Inc. ("happy").

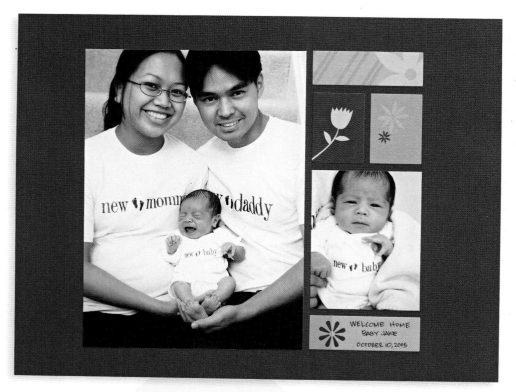

Welcome Home
by Aimee Fernandez-Capina

Showcasing their new T-shirts and roles, the Fernandez-Capina family cuddled close for a homecoming photo session.

TIP: Create an instant classic by converting color photos to black-and-white.

SOURCES Cardstock: Bazzill Basics Paper. Stickers: Scrapworks. Pen: Zig Writer by EK Success. Photos: Joy Uzarraga.

Turn up the heat on your design. Stamp words with embossing ink and sprinkle on clear powder for a tone-on-tone effect when melted.

New Mama   by Kelly Noel

Kelly chose a photo that shows her securing her new baby in the car seat to match her reflections on her new role as protector and parent.

TIP: Make your page more meaningful to your child by composing journaling as though you're writing to the baby.

SOURCES Cardstock: Bazzill Basics Paper. Patterned paper: KI Memories. Stickers: KI Memories. Chipboard letters: Heidi Swapp. Pen: Sharpie.

Life has changed so much since having you! In my social work career, at one point I was responsible for over 60 children! Life was busy, hectic and very stressful. I worked long hours and very rarely got any reward for my hard work. How lucky am I now that I get to stay home and be with you all day?! Sure, life is still busy and hectic and I definitely work long hours— But the reward is so much more … caring for you the best way I know how and seeing you grow and thrive makes me the happiest new mama in the world!

new mama

Although, we've been through this before, it still is a challenge. Figuring out sleeping patterns, allergies, food preferences. You would think that these little things would come with a "How To" Manual, but instead we are left on our own to figure it all out. We make mistakes, we keep trying. It's what parenting is all about. This time around I see a more confident you. You are comfortable holding Jimmy and rocking him to sleep. You are more than willing to give him a bottle or change his diaper. I so appreciate the father you are to James and the father you are to Katelyn and Joey. We are all blessed. You make us laugh, you keep us calm, you relax us. I think you are an amazing father and there isn't another person that I would want on this adventure called "Parenting."

Our Adventure by Jennifer Gallacher

Armed with a single photo of her husband and newborn son, Jennifer created this colorful tribute to her husband's parenting skills.

TIP: Small bits of busy patterned paper can go a long way. Jennifer used a strip along the bottom to anchor her title.

SOURCES Cardstock: Bazzill Basics Paper. Patterned paper, charms, paper clips: Karen Foster Design. Font: Antique Type off the Internet. Chipboard letter, ribbon, rickrack: Li'l Davis Designs. Stickers: Arctic Frog (alphabet), Karen Foster Design (buttons). Punch: McGill Inc.

> Purchase the *supplies* for a certain page together, and then **store** them in a page protector with the photos. When you get time to scrapbook, the first step is *done!*
>
> Jen Lessinger, 2006 Creative Team member

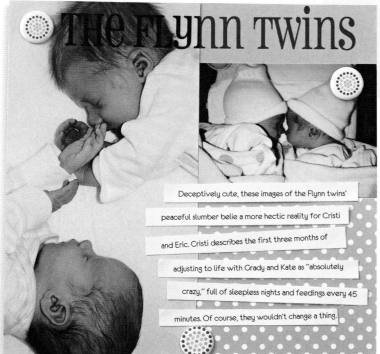

Deceptively cute, these images of the Flynn twins' peaceful slumber belie a more hectic reality for Cristi and Eric. Cristi describes the first three months of adjusting to life with Grady and Kate as "absolutely crazy," full of sleepless nights and feedings every 45 minutes. Of course, they wouldn't change a thing.

The Flynn Twins by Michelle Rubin

After seeing these photos of her friend's newborn twins, Michelle made this 6x6" page as part of a gift album.

TIP: Embellish your embellishments. Rub-ons are great for adding an extra creative touch to other accents, like the brads on this page.

SOURCES Cardstock, patterned paper: Making Memories. Font: Pharmacy (title), Eurofurence (journaling) off the Internet. Rub-ons: Autumn Leaves. Brads: Bazzill Basics Paper.

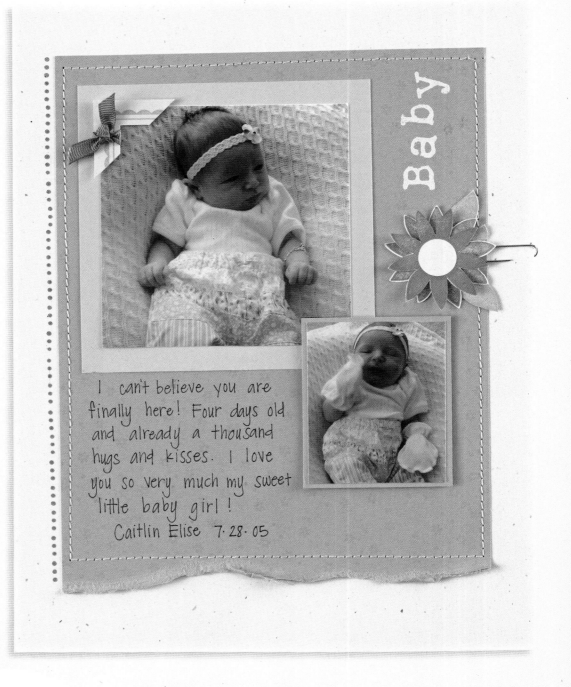

I can't believe you are finally here! Four days old and already a thousand hugs and kisses. I love you so very much my sweet little baby girl!
Caitlin Elise 7·28·05

 Keep handwritten journaling straight by marking light guidelines with a pencil and ruler. Erase them when done writing.

Baby by Emily Call

Emily took a cue from her daughter's ensemble for the powdery pastels and flower accent on this page.

TIP: Give a basic design a little oomph by stamping a pattern—like the small dots on this page—down one side.

SOURCES Cardstock, stamps, ink, embossing powder: Stampin' Up!.

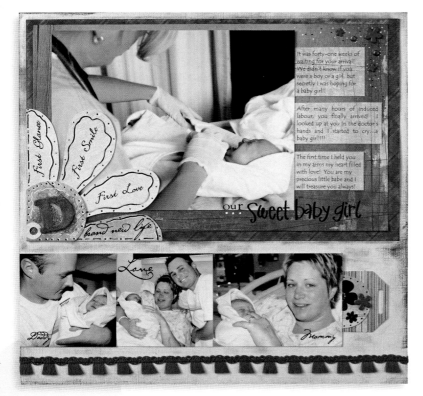

Our Sweet Baby Girl by Vicki Boutin

Surprised by her newborn's gender, Vicki was oh-so happy she got the chance to use pink on this page.

TIP: Snip scraps of cardstock and patterned paper into simple shapes to create your accent for pennies.

SOURCES Cardstock: Bazzill Basics Paper. Patterned paper, tags: BasicGrey. Rub-ons: Scenic Route Paper Co. (on petals), Déjà Views for The C-Thru Ruler Co. (title). Rubber stamps: Scraptivity. Ink: Tsukineko. Chipboard letter: Li'l Davis Designs. Brads: Making Memories. Pens: Sanford (white gel), Sakura of America (black). Trim: Venus Industries. Beads: Provo Craft.

Instead of searching through tons of *fonts* for each layout, choose *two or three* simple fonts to use with anything.

Leah Fung, contributing editor

BABY'S FIRST PICTURES

When Mom goes into labor, the trip to the hospital is often quite hectic. But keeping these few tips in mind as you head out the door will help you make your baby's delivery picture perfect.

• **Shoot before the show starts.** Mom may think she looks awful, but the moments before Baby arrives are memorable. Someday she'll appreciate those hospital shots and fondly recall the excitement of that day.

• **Have the camera ready.** In the heat of the moment, you don't want to be scrambling around looking for your gear. Bring a camera that's easily stashed in a pocket to be pulled out in time to catch that once-in-a-lifetime shot.

• **Look for flattering angles.** Shots taken over the doctor's shoulder at the moment of birth aren't always album-worthy, but that doesn't mean you should miss the moment. A spot right near Mom's shoulder is the perfect vantage point to capture Baby being towelled off on Mom's tummy. Lots of doctors will even hold the baby up right after delivery for a not-to-be-missed shot.

• **Enlist help.** Although safety is the first priority, nurses are often willing to take photos of the family with the newborn, wait an extra moment for Dad to snap a picture, or even point out a good shot. They want this time to be as memorable as you do.

Set your camera to a low f-stop to focus in on Baby's hand, foot, or other tiny part, and to blur out the foreground and background in the photo.

New by Sarah Klemish

Sarah captured the beauty of her newborn baby by taking a sweet close-up photo of one of her hands. To balance the page, she used thin strips of patterned paper to add color without overwhelming the photo.

TIP: Trim elements from die-cut paper to add interest to your page. Sarah used a vertical strip from a sheet of die-cut butterflies to make it appear as if they are fluttering up the page.

SOURCES Cardstock: Bazzill Basics Paper. Patterned paper: October Afternoon (newsprint, stripe), BoBunny Press (pink dot), KI Memories (die-cut butterflies). Chipboard letters and buttons: BasicGrey. Font: Uncle Charles by Autumn Leaves. Die cut: Crate Paper. Punch: Stampin' Up!.

A NEW baby is like the BEGINNING of all things - wonder, HOPE, a dream of possibilities.

Eda J. Leshan

new

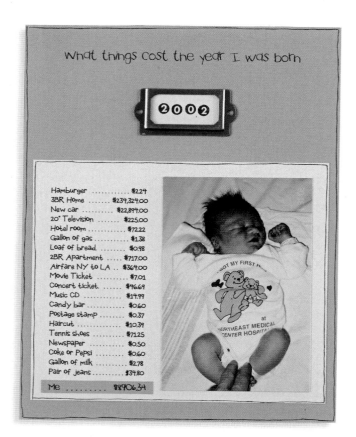

What things cost the year I was born

2002

Hamburger	$2.24
3BR Home	$234,324.00
New car	$22,894.00
20" Television	$225.00
Hotel room	$72.22
Gallon of gas	$1.38
Loaf of bread	$0.98
2BR Apartment	$717.00
Airfare NY to LA	$364.00
Movie Ticket	$7.01
Concert ticket	$46.69
Music CD	$19.99
Candy bar	$0.60
Postage stamp	$0.37
Haircut	$10.39
Tennis shoes	$71.25
Newspaper	$0.50
Coke or Pepsi	$0.60
Gallon of milk	$2.78
Pair of jeans	$34.80
Me	$8906.34

What Things Cost by Jennifer Miller

An informative—yet still fun—page about the year Jennifer's baby was born is bound to be an album favorite as the years go by.

TIP: Add a year-in-review page to your baby's book. Twenty years from now, it will help both of you remember life back then.

SOURCES Cardstock: Bazzill Basics Paper. Font: Sandbox (title), Tuxedo (journaling) by Two Peas in a Bucket. Rubber stamps: PSX. Ink: Ranger Industries. Pen: Zig Writer by EK Success. Label holder: Li'l Davis Designs.

> When an *idea* for a page comes to you, jot it down or *sketch* it out on an index card and store it with the *photos* you want to use. Then you won't need to *hunt* for photos when you're *ready* for that page!
>
> Leslie Lightfoot, 2005 Creative Team member

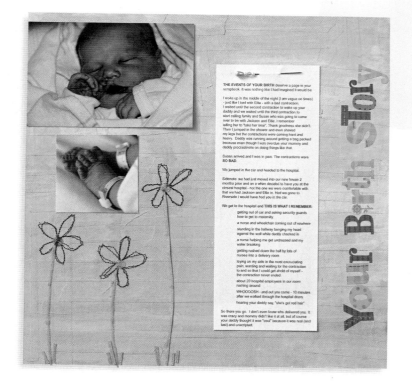

Your Birth Story

Your Birth Story by Cathy Blackstone

Cathy created this page to share with her daughter the story of her speedy entry into the world.

TIP: Take creative license with your background. Cathy covered her page with masking tape and brightened it with acrylic paint for an unusual, textural look.

$ **SOURCES** Font: Arial. Stickers: K&Company. Sequins: Hero Arts. Pins: Making Memories.

We welcome with love

Brynn Katherine

9 pounds, 13 ounces   December 30th
21 inches   8:29 a.m.

Cathy and Brad Blackstone

Brynn Katherine
by Cathy Blackstone

Small touches like a patterned paper, some ribbon, and a diaper pin go a long way in jazzing up a simple, easily replicated design.

SOURCES Patterned paper: My Mind's Eye. Font: Bickely Script (script), Helvetica Neue (print). Ribbon: KI Memories.

Classification: Cute

by Michelle Rubin

Look to precut cards, tags, pockets, and mini folders to simplify the process of mass production. Or make cutting easier with the help of a die and a die-cutting tool.

SOURCES Mini folder: Provo Craft. Cardstock: Bazzill Basics Paper. Font: Typo by Two Peas in a Bucket. Clip: Making Memories.

Classification: Cute

Name: Lilly Marie Bauer
Birth date: Feb. 24, 2006
Description: 6 lbs., 9 oz.,
20 inches
Accomplices: Claire & Bill
(a.k.a. Mom & Dad)

Subject is under
investigation for being
excessively adorable. She is
reportedly packing a lethal
dose of cuteness and has
been seen sleeping, eating,
and cuddling in the area.
Subject should be handled
with excessive caution
and fawning when spotted.

We are thrilled to
announce the arrival of

Griffin Phillip Reimer

August, 12, 2005
8 pounds, 6 ounces
21 inches

Susan and Phil

Griffin
by Cathy Blackstone

This square baby announcement is easy to make in mass quantities. One 12 × 12" sheet of cardstock will yield four 3 × 3" announcements. Just remember that square and other odd shapes often require more postage. Check with your post office before mailing.

SOURCES Patterned paper: My Mind's Eye. Fonts: Weathered Fence (name) by Two Peas in a Bucket, Helvetica Neu Light (details) off the Internet. Ribbon: Making Memories.

Brendan
by Michelle Rubin

Make room for a large photo by adding all of the new baby's information to the photo's empty spaces with image-editing software. For a 5 × 5" gatefold card such as this one, cut a 10×5" strip and score fold marks 2½" in from both sides.

SOURCES Software: Adobe Photoshop Elements. Fonts: Pharmacy (name) off the Internet, Century Gothic (details). Charm: Making Memories.

ANNOUNCEMENTS MADE EASY

Finding the time to create handmade announcements can be tricky once Baby is a part of your daily routine. The keys to getting it all done: good planning and doing as much as possible ahead of time.

• **Create a design.** Don't wait until your little one arrives to find the ideal paper and embellishments. Not sure if you're having a girl or a boy? Choose gender-neutral embellishments and paper color, such as sage green, so you can do most of the work beforehand.

• **Do a trial run.** Craft a sample card so you know the correct sizes and products to use and any trouble spots that need to be smoothed out. Leave room for the essentials—the baby's name, size, and birth date.

• **Gather supplies.** Purchase the paper, cardstock, adhesives, embellishments, and envelopes you'll need, plus extras in case of mistakes. (Remember to keep an announcement for your scrapbook.) Buy postage stamps.

• **Address envelopes in advance.** Track down the addresses of friends who have moved.

• **Consider other options.** If you have a long list of friends and relatives, it may be impractical to make a card for everyone. Scanning your announcement and e-mailing it allows you to share your joy with lots of people at once, and it saves time and money. The important thing is to introduce your new family member to those you care about and who care about you.

visitor album

Record the rush of well-wishers arriving to greet the newborn with a special scrapbook. Candi Gershon whipped up a quick visitor album to show her new nephew how many people were eager to meet him.

1. Before the baby is born, cut cardstock journaling blocks and take them to the hospital (or send them with the parents-to-be).

2. After the baby arrives, take a photo of each visitor with the baby, and ask him or her to write a message to be included in the book.

3. Pair the photos and messages and mount them on simple backgrounds. Keep it easy by picking simple embellishments. With a small album like this one, you don't have to add much!

SOURCES Album: We R Memory Keepers. Patterned paper, die cuts, wood frame: Chatterbox. Rub-ons: BasicGrey (footprint), My Mind's Eye ("grandpa & me"). Stickers: SEI. Buttons: Junkitz ("grandparent"), Autumn Leaves (other). Brad: K&Company. Ribbon, safety pin: Making Memories. Metal accents: Making Memories (handprint), EK Success (heart). Chipboard accents: Making Memories (heart), Heidi Swapp ("uncle"). Monogram: My Mind's Eye. Design: Candi Gershon.

A 6x6" album is the perfect size for pages featuring 4x6" photos.

Dear Finley,
Gracie and I were so excited to find out we had a baby brother! We waited for you for *so* long. The wait was worth it. You are so cute! We love you with all of our hearts, baby brother!
Love,
Hannah and Gracie

a brother to love

Help guests write straight by lightly drawing lines in pencil.

grandpa&me

Finn,
    When I saw you for the first time I noticed immediately that you were very smart, extremely good looking and had a great personality! You obviously take after your grandpa Cosley.
I love you little buddy.
Grandpa Cosley

Look for family-themed accents, such as the rub-on here, that become ready-made titles.

Dear Finn,
    When I first saw you I thought to myself, "What a handsome little man!" I look forward to all the fun memories we are going to share. I _love_ you so very much and I am honored to be apart of your life!

        Love Always,
        Your Uncle Ryan

UNCLE

If you create the design in advance, make the photo spaces 4x6" for a perfect fit.

grandpa

Yo FINLEY,

WELCOME ON BOARD! I CAN'T WAIT UNTIL YOU GROW UP SO WE CAN PLAY BALL TOGETHER. I LIKE TO PLAY SOFTBALL, BASKETBALL AND RIDE MY BIKE. MAYBE WHEN YOU GET BIGGER, YOU CAN RIDE YOUR BIKE WITH ME. ONE OF MY FAVORITE KINDS OF FOODS IS JELLY BELLIES IN ALL KINDS OF FLAVORS. I LIKE THEM A LOT BECAUSE THEY HAVE NO FAT AND I CAN EAT ALL I WANT. ANOTHER FAVORITE OF MINE IS VANILLA ICE CREAM AND POPSICLES. I CAN EAT A BOX AT A TIME. BEFORE I FORGET, CHICKEN WINGS ARE ANOTHER FAVORITE OF MINE. I CLEAN THE MEAT DOWN TO THE BONE. (ASK GRANDMA) I LOVE FOOD ALOT AND THAT'S WHY I HAVE TO WORKOUT SO MUCH. I HOPE THAT YOU GROW UP TO BE BIG AND STRONG SO WE CAN HANG OUT.
LOVE YA,
GRANDPA - CHEZ

For easy layouts, make some journaling blocks large enough to fill a page.

brag book

Share your big news in a small album that you can take everywhere. Renee Villalobos-Campa showcased photos of her daughter in a customizable mini binder that looks intricate, but is easy to assemble thanks to mix-and-match components like divider tabs, pocket pages, and envelopes.

1. Plan out the sequence of pages: How do you want your story to unfold? Renee started with her daughter's birth details, then went on to meeting the family and going home.

2. Adhere patterned paper to each page, then add photos, journaling, and embellishments. Know in advance how many photos will fit on each page of your mini album so you don't waste time cropping too many shots.

3. Decorate the cover of the album. Adhere patterned paper, or paint the cover; then dress it up with photos and accents. Seal the cover with decoupage medium so it will withstand all the attention it will no doubt receive. Renee added an elastic band to keep hers closed, but you could wrap yours with a single strand of ribbon.

SOURCES Binder, insert pages: Hot off the Press. Patterned paper: Autumn Leaves. Fonts: Steelfish off the Internet. Acrylic paint: Delta. Flower, ribbon: Michaels. Buttons: Junkitz. Clips, brads: Provo Craft. Tags: Avery Dennison. Design: Renee Villalobos-Campa.

Blank album materials make it easy to personalize your brag book.

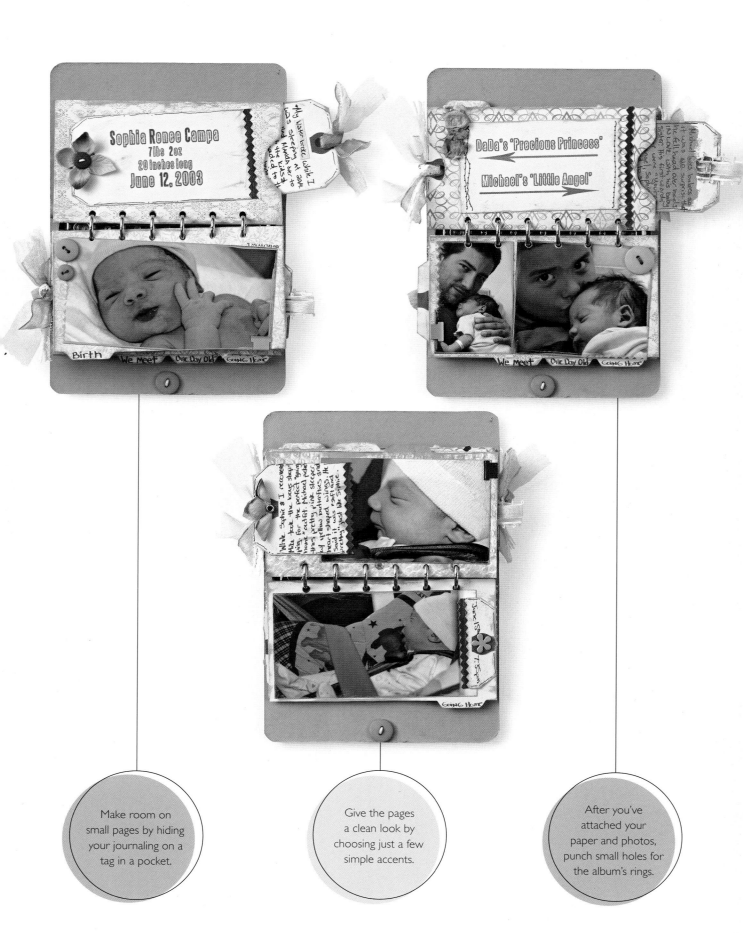

Make room on small pages by hiding your journaling on a tag in a pocket.

Give the pages a clean look by choosing just a few simple accents.

After you've attached your paper and photos, punch small holes for the album's rings.

IT'S A FIRST! THE FIRST bath, first word, and first step are just a few of the big moments in your baby's life. Milestones are the highlights of any baby book, but the trick is to capture them when they happen. Babies grow and change so quickly you need to be on your toes if you want to preserve those precious memories.

Milestones
& development

Buy "raw" or unfinished chipboard accents and use paint, ink, or patterned paper to give them a makeover to match your color scheme.

Head's Up by Sandi Hicks

Sandi layered three patterned papers in similar hues to make a page highlighting her daughter's newfound ability to hold her head up.

TIP: Stitch a casual border around the edges of any layout. If you don't have a sewing machine, hand-stitch or fake it with rub-ons.

SOURCES Cardstock: Bazzill Basics Paper. Patterned paper: Autumn Leaves (paisley), Melissa Frances (dot, stripe). Pen: EK Success. Chipboard accents: Heidi Swapp. Ribbon: All My Memories (rickrack, check), May Arts (stripe). Button, brads: Making Memories.

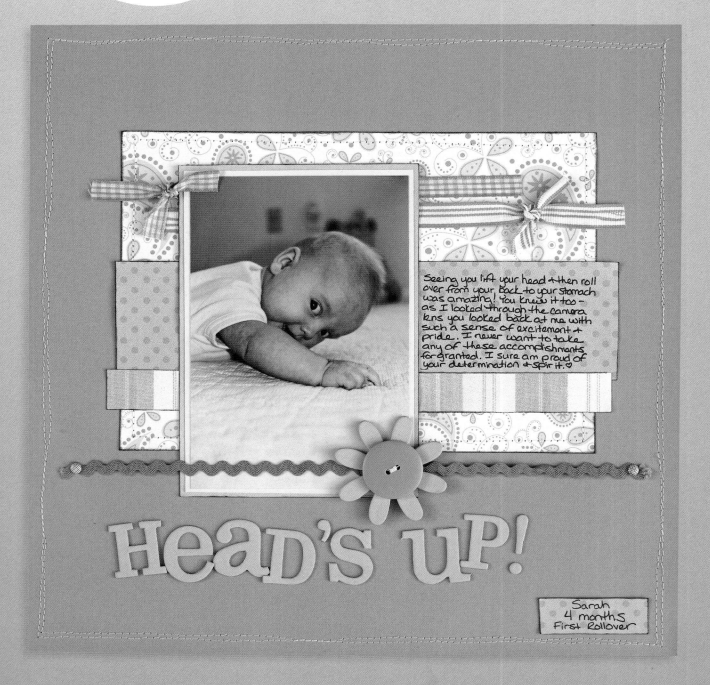

Seeing you lift your head + then roll over from your back to your stomach was amazing! You knew it too - as I looked through the camera lens you looked back at me with such a sense of excitement + pride. I never want to take any of these accomplishments for granted. I sure am proud of your determination + spirit. ♥

HEAD'S UP!

Sarah
4 months
First Rollover

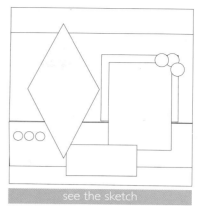

see the sketch

One Little Lock by Jessica Sprague

When Jessica's daughter had her first haircut, Mom saved a single golden curl and paired it with a black-and-white photo for a lasting keepsake.

TIP: Preserve mementos, like locks of hair, on your pages by tucking them into see-through bags or envelopes.

SOURCES Patterned paper, flowers, brads, ribbon, photo corner: Chatterbox. Fonts: Myriad (journaling) by Adobe, Impact (pink text) off the Internet. Stickers: American Crafts. Rub-ons: Autumn Leaves (flourish), 7Gypsies ("limited edition"), Heidi Swapp ("one little").

10 Months of Smiles by Sheila Doherty

By numbering each photo on this spread about her son's 10 months of smiles, Sheila made it easy for the eye to travel from one month to the next.

TIP: Show growth and change in your baby's life with photos taken at different stages and that follow a common theme.

SOURCES Cardstock: Prism Papers. Patterned paper: KI Memories. Font: Century Gothic. Stickers: Chatterbox. Rub-ons, brads: Making Memories. Wood accent: Li'l Davis Designs. Ribbon: Michaels.

five
months

08.30.05 shots (you did so well!)
09.05.05 slept 8:30pm-6am!
09.05.05 slept on your belly part of the night
09.12.05 flew to Pennsylvania to see Grandma &
         Grandpa Killins
09.13.05 said 'ma' when you were upset
09.20.05 sat up in your bouncer to eat the pole
09.21.05 sat in highchair & drank from sippy cup
09.23.05 went to the doctor for that spider bite

- 5 month weight/height: 20lbs.1oz./26.25in.
- Nursing 8 times a day
- Blowing raspberries
- Gummy smile
- Definitely a hip baby
- Alla-Balla, Honey Bunny
- Leaning toward us to be held
- Reaching for my breast when I lay you down
  beside me

Pressed for time? Create a page for each month that features key details. That way, you can spend as little or as much time scrapbooking as you'd like.

Five Months by J.J. Killins

To support the cheerful photo of her daughter Alla at 5 months, J. J. pulled a list of dates from a calendar on which she had briefly noted all the little things she knew she would forget if she didn't write them down.

TIP: Coordinate all the layouts about your baby's monthly milestones by sticking with the same basic design and just varying the colors and embellishments.

SOURCES Cardstock: Bazzill Basics Paper. Patterned paper: Urban Lily. Fonts: Texas Hero ("months"), Stomp Duality (journaling) off the Internet, Times New Roman ("five"). Die cut: Colorbök. Ribbon: SEI (pink flowers), Offray (wide pink).

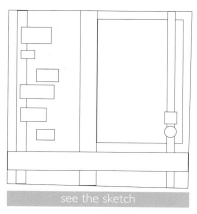

see the sketch

Crawl by Jennifer Bourgeault

Once her daughter started walking, Jennifer created this tribute to a passing phase—crawling—with a shot that perfectly captured the moment.

TIP: Journal about a photo from the past with a new perspective you may have gained since it was taken.

SOURCES Patterned paper: Me and My Big Ideas (floral), Fontwerks (blue plaid). Font: Avant Garde off the Internet. Stickers, metal frames: Junkitz. Acrylic accents: Heidi Swapp. Acrylic paint: Making Memories.

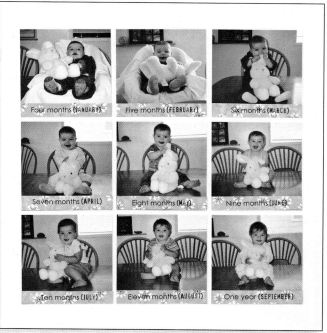

The Incredible Shrinking Bunny by Leigh Penner

Leigh charted her daughter's growth through her first year by taking her photo with the same stuffed animal every month. By the end, the bunny seemed so much smaller than in the newborn photo.

TIP: When putting many photos on one layout, try cropping them all the same size and shape and lining them up in a grid to keep the design crisp and clean.

SOURCES Patterned paper: Chatterbox. Fonts: Hootie (title) off the Internet, Century Gothic ("the incredible," journaling, dates). Brads: Making Memories.

Mix and match leftover sticker, chipboard, and acrylic letters to spell out a title in a fun and colorful way.

Tactile   by Jen Lessinger

Inspired by her son's favorite plaything, Jen paired photos with textural accents to reflect her son's growing awareness of the world around him.

TIP: Let a photo or other flat element pop off the page by attaching it with adhesive foam. Jen gave the smaller photo more prominence by raising it.

SOURCES Cardstock: Bazzill Basics Paper. Patterned paper: K&Company (teal), Autumn Leaves (orange). Font: Century Gothic. Chipboard accents: Scenic Route Paper Co. (green square, "i"), Heidi Swapp (hearts, "a," "e," "L"). Acrylic accents: KI Memories. Ribbon: American Crafts.

Your awareness of the world around you is growing every day, G. And your ability to connect with that world is growing, too. Reaching, touching, grasping, feeling. You are all about the tactile stuff. This little toy was a gift from June and Mark for being the honorary ring bearer in their wedding. I am not sure if it is the color or the face that fascinates you, but you will go to extreme baby measures to get your hands on it. Yesterday, you slid and rolled six feet across the living room as I was doing dishes, all for your little doo dad.

JUL 0 5

tactile

3 by Kelly Stocksen

Kelly paired serious-feeling papers with a joyful photo of her daughter as she recounted her bittersweet feelings about her baby growing out of the newborn stage.

TIP: Use the empty space in an enlarged photo to display your title. Here, you still get a hint of the baby's body without sacrificing space for the title.

 SOURCES Patterned paper: 7Gypsies. Fonts: Hannibal Lector ("three months"), Tahoma (journaling) off the Internet. Ribbon: Offray.

Let *older* kids *help* you with your scrapbooking. Simply placing *photos* can make them feel they're part of the *process*.

Helen Naylor, 2004 Creative Team member

10 Months by Brenda Carpenter

After photographing her daughter Audrey playing with some silk flowers, Brenda placed the blooms on a layout describing her daughter at 10 months.

TIP: Dress up your pages with everyday items, like these silk flowers. Then find fun ways of blending them into your page, as Brenda did by journaling on cut paper leaves.

SOURCES Cardstock, brads: Bazzill Basics Paper. Patterned paper, stickers: Scenic Route Paper Co. Font: Uncle Charles by Autumn Leaves. Foam stamp: Li'l Davis Designs. Ink: Clearsnap. Ribbon: May Arts. Flowers: Michaels. Pen, punch: Stampin' Up!.

For a story-telling series, use your camera's continuous shooting feature to capture your little one's attempts to roll over, crawl, or walk.

Stand, Step, Crash by Jen Lessinger

Jen took a step-by-step approach to this layout about her son just learning to walk, choosing oversize sticker letters for her three-part title.

TIP: Stack photos shot in sequence for a filmstrip effect that shows the progression of movement or a change over time.

SOURCES Cardstock: DMD Industries (white), Bazzill Basics Paper (brown). Patterned paper: Scenic Route Paper Co. (teal), BasicGrey (orange). Font: American Typewriter. Stickers: American Crafts. Tag: Avery Dennison. Chipboard accents: Heidi Swapp.

stand

It's a process, this walking thing.
First you have to learn to stand.

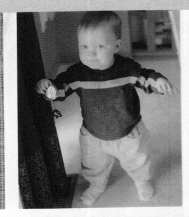

step

Then you have to take that step.
It's a leap of faith, really.

crash

And then there is the crash.
It happens. Often.

G — almost 11 mo.

Rolling on the Floor by Kim Haynes

Kim cropped a floral-print paper into large circles to create a clever layout about her daughter's new skills.

TIP: Alter accents to fit your layout's needs. Kim cut apart a woven label because the entire sentiment ("rolling on the floor laughing") didn't fit her theme. She trimmed off the word "laughing," and the remainder worked perfectly as her title.

SOURCES Patterned paper: American Crafts. Ink: Ranger Industries. Woven label: Me and My Big Ideas.

First Bath by Aimee Fernandez-Capina

Aimee took a step-by-step approach to scrapbooking her baby's first bath by printing each numbered step right beneath the photo.

TIP: Convert newborn photos to black-and-white for a timeless look and to minimize a newborn's blotchy skin.

SOURCES Cardstock: Bazzil Basics Paper. Patterned paper, rub-ons: Autumn Leaves. Font: Jack Frost by Two Peas in a Bucket.

Take the guess-work out of mixing patterned paper by choosing from a manufacturer's already coordinated line.

Teething Flower by Nely Fok

By running her title vertically and tightly cropping her photos, Nely was able to fit lots in on this page about her daughter's teething habits.

TIP: Select a patterned paper that helps emphasize your theme. Nely chose a floral-pattern paper to go with photos and journaling about her baby's teething flower, but she downplayed the busy print by bookending it with a bold stripe.

SOURCES Patterned paper: Chatterbox. Font: Times New Roman. Chipboard accents: Heidi Swapp. Label holder, brads: Queen & Co. Sequins: Doodlebug Design.

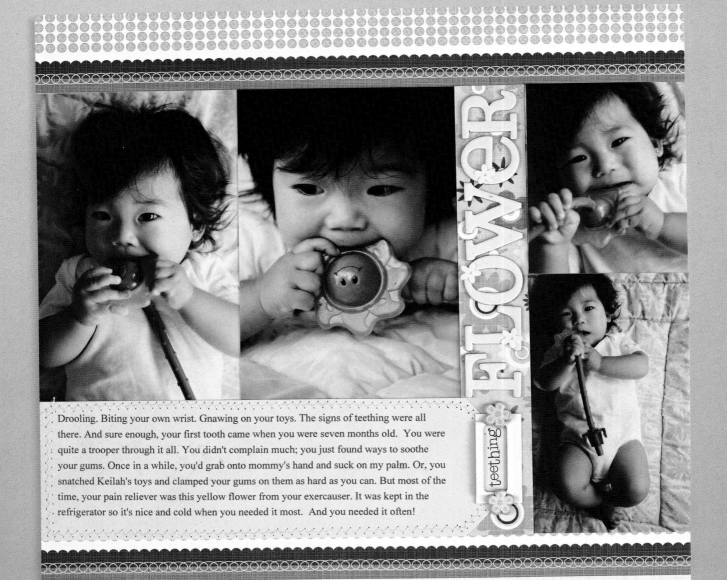

Drooling. Biting your own wrist. Gnawing on your toys. The signs of teething were all there. And sure enough, your first tooth came when you were seven months old. You were quite a trooper through it all. You didn't complain much; you just found ways to soothe your gums. Once in a while, you'd grab onto mommy's hand and suck on my palm. Or, you snatched Keilah's toys and clamped your gums on them as hard as you can. But most of the time, your pain reliever was this yellow flower from your exercauser. It was kept in the refrigerator so it's nice and cold when you needed it most. And you needed it often!

FLOWER

teething

6-month MILESTONES

- ☐ Weight: 17 lbs. 15 oz.
- ☐ Height: 27 1/2"
- ☐ First Food: Rice Cereal (YUM!) August 11, 2004
- ☐ First Fruit: Apples (SOUR!) August 25, 2004
- ☐ First Veggies: Sweet Potatoes (YUM!) August 31, 2004
- ☐ Sat Alone August 16, 2004
- ☐ First Tooth (Bottom Right) August 12, 2004
- ☐ Second Tooth (Bottom Left) August 13, 2004
- ☐ Third Tooth (Top Right) September 6, 2004
- ☐ Fourth Tooth (Top Left) September 16, 2004
- ☐ Stole Mommy's Heart EVERYDAY!

6-Month Milestones by Sheila Doherty

Sheila combined bright colors and black-and-white photos in a simple design to highlight the major milestones her son had accomplished at 6 months old.

TIP: Try bullet journaling on monthly layouts to highlight key events. Keeping the design simple when you have lots of information to cover will make it easier to follow.

$ SOURCES Patterned paper: Scrapworks (polka dot), KI Memories (heart). Font: Rockwell off the Internet. Brads: Making Memories. Bottle cap: Li'l Davis Designs. Ribbon: American Crafts.

8 Months by Kim Heffington

Kim kept the focus on her beautiful photos with a simple layout that consists of cardstock, a hand-cut title, and heartfelt journaling.

TIP: If you have several cute photos, crop them creatively so you can include more. Repeating the same-size square keeps this page from looking too jumbled.

SOURCES Font: Century Gothic. Pen: EK Success.

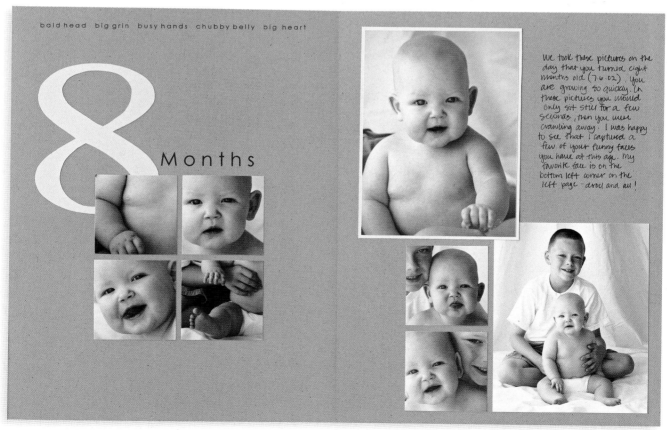

bald head big grin busy hands chubby belly big heart

8 Months

We took these pictures on the day that you turned eight months old (7.6.02). You are growing so quickly. In these pictures you would only sit still for a few seconds, then you were crawling away. I was happy to see that I captured a few of your funny faces you have at this age. My favorite face is on the bottom left corner on the left page - drool and all!

Tiptoes by April Peterson

One photo and a simple design help April remember her son's newfound skill of stretching to reach things.

TIP: Don't be afraid to use pink and flowers on layouts about boys. They evoke a softness that goes well with babies of either gender.

 SOURCES Cardstock: Bazzill Basics Paper. Patterned paper: SEI. Font: Mank-Sans off the Internet. Rub-ons: Doodlebug Design. Ink: Hero Arts.

Cherish by Kim Heffington

When her daughter turned 1 year, Kim set up her own photo shoot—complete with a cute head wreath as a prop—and made the photos the focus of her layout.

TIP: To make your own backdrop for a do-it-yourself portrait session, attach a solid-color sheet or drop cloth to a wall and let it drape down onto the floor.

SOURCES Decorative paper: Artistic Scrapper. Sticker: K&Company. Ink: Stampa Rosa. Pen: EK Success. Safety pin, tag, rub-on: Making Memories. Chalk: Craf-T Products.

Arms extended, he reaches and stretches
for the object that has caught his eye.
His fingers just barely miss and without pause he is on his tiptoes.
It is a new skill and just weeks ago would have been impossible,
but now it is routine.
With that little extra height
his fingers snatch the object and he is pleased.

10.10.2004

The world just got a half-inch smaller.

We had a little fun with your one year portrait session. The wreath on your head was a project I learned how to do from the internet. It was a good idea at the time ♥ You still look absolutely adorable despite the wreath. and as you can see in a few of these pics you couldn't wait to get it off your bald, little head!

cherish

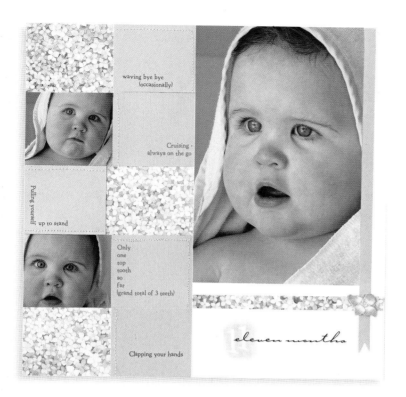

waving bye bye
(occasionally)

Cruising -
always on the go

Pulling yourself
up to stand

Only
one
top
tooth
so
far
(grand total of 3 teeth)

Clapping your hands

eleven months

11 Months   by Joy Bollinger

Joy typed short summaries of her baby's achievements in the 11th month on blocks of cardstock she later stitched to the layout.

TIP: Use stickers as stencils or masks. Joy gently removed the "11" stickers in her title after chalking over them for a muted embellishment to her title.

SOURCES Patterned paper: Colors by Design. Fonts: Carpenter ICG (title) off the Internet, Chestnuts (journaling) by Two Peas in a Bucket. Stickers: K&Company (flower), Creative Imaginations ("11"). Chalk: Craft-T Products.

A great way to scrap miscellaneous photos is to *create monthly* pages summarizing milestones and memories.

Lisa Storms, 2006 Creative Team member

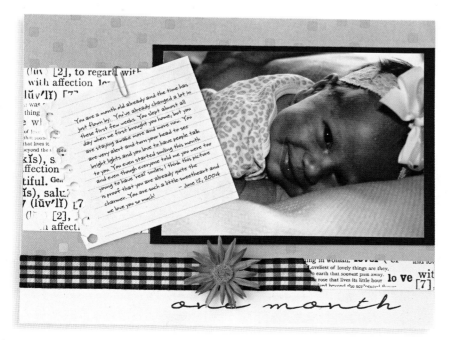

You are a month old already and the time has just flown by. You've already changed a lot in these first few weeks. You slept almost all day when we first brought you home, but you are staying awake more and more now. You are very alert and turn your head to have people talk to you. You even started smiling this month and even though everyone told me you were too young to have 'real' smiles, I think this picture is proof that you are already quite the charmer. You are such a little sweetheart and we love you so much!   — June 12, 2004

one month

One Month   by Kelly Stocksen

Kelly used one large photo and a simple block of journaling to mark her daughter's first month.

TIP: Compose your journaling as though it is a letter to your child. Years from now, your child will love reading your words of love.

SOURCES Patterned paper: KI Memories (pink), 7Gypsies (text). Font: Piano Recital (journaling) by Two Peas in a Bucket. Ribbon: Offray.

You Are Growing So Fast
by Jill Godon

Multiple photos from her son's first year and extensive journaling record how fast that year went by for Jill.

TIP: Using your computer, resize a group of photos to fit the available space. On this layout, Jill fit 24 photos and still had plenty of room to journal.

SOURCES Cardstock: Bazzill Basics Paper. Patterned paper: Chatterbox. Fonts: SP Purkage (title) off the Internet, Century Gothic (journaling). Rub-ons: Imagination Project. Chipboard accents, acrylic paint: Making Memories. Ribbon: American Crafts.

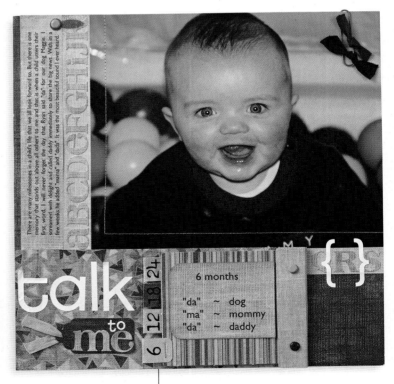

Talk to Me
by Dana Smith

To keep track of her son's growing vocabulary, Dana added a mini album to her page with plans to insert more pages as he learns new words.

TIP: Use a kit to create a mini album that can be attached to your page. Dana kept the look cohesive by using one from the same manufacturer as her patterned paper.

SOURCES Patterned paper, album kit, tag: BasicGrey. Font: Gill Sans. Stickers: BasicGrey (alphabet, "me"), American Crafts ("talk," brackets). Ink: Ranger Industries. Rub-ons: Making Memories. Brads: Carolee's Creations. Twill: Scenic Route Paper Co. Paper clip: Junkitz.

you can pull yourself to a stand. // you eat some table food, but mostly baby food. // you wake up in the middle of the night fairly often. // you are fast. I had forgotten how quickly a baby can crawl. // you are almost 22 pounds and 29.5 inches long. // you like most foods but not baby food mac & cheese. //

Nine-Month Milestones

by Jen Lessinger

For quick journaling about her son's development at 9 months, Jen made a short list of facts and stats.

TIP: Enlarge a favorite photo to 8x10" to make a quick and simple page.

$ SOURCES Cardstock: DMD Industries (white), Bazzill Basics Paper (red). Patterned paper: American Crafts (multicolor), BasicGrey (distressed). Chipboard letters: Heidi Swapp.

Could They Be Cuter?

by Melissa Diekema

Melissa used a brad to attach a cardstock strip that rotates to reveal hidden journaling on this page about a friend's twin boys.

TIP: Add interest to your title by mixing letter stickers and stamps. Stamp letters on white cardstock and cut them out so you don't have to fear making mistakes that can creep in when hand-lettering.

SOURCES Cardstock: Bazzill Basics Paper. Rub-ons: KI Memories. Stickers: American Crafts. Stamps: Fontwerks. Ink: Stampin' Up! (blue), Clearsnap (red). Brads, photo turns: Making Memories. Label maker: Dymo.

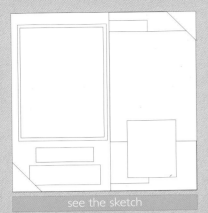

see the sketch

Solid Eater by Candi Gershon

On this design Candi supported great in-the-moment photos of her daughter with journaling about the process of making the switch to solid foods.

TIP: Add a layer of vellum to tone down patterned paper and create a cool effect. Candi used it as a mat to help her photo and title stand out.

SOURCES Cardstock, patterned paper: SEI. Fonts: Garamouche by P22 (journaling), Scrap Cursive ("solid") off the Internet. Chipboard accents: Li'l Davis Designs.

The switch to solid foods was an easy one. You seemed to show interest in our food pretty quickly after we started feeding you jarred foods. You have an appetite your brother has never had. We joke that you are the human vacuum cleaner. When we started giving you the Gerber vanilla cereal squares, we knew we had found a winner. You would not settle for one or two or even five, no, you needed at least ten at a time. I have tasted the little squares myself, and I agree that they are pretty good in comparison to the mashed green beans in a jar that you ate prior. But, I also think the fun for you was feeding yourself. The little squares are just the size for your tiny hands to hold. You would shovel them into your mouth and Daddy and I would have to remind you that one at a time is plenty. This switch to not only solid foods, but now finger foods, has been a messy one, but we have enjoyed every minute of it. It's just another mark of your independence (now that you don't need Daddy and I to hand feed you every meal). It's also another reminder of how big my baby girl is getting!

11/23/03

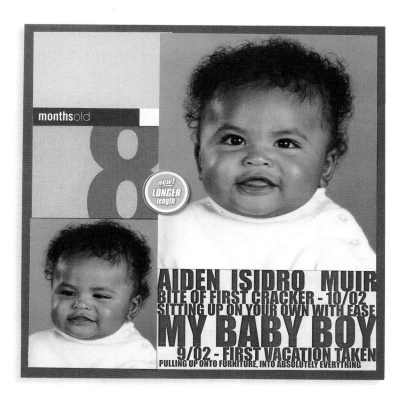

8 Months Old   by Nia Reddy

Nia turned text about her son's 8th month into a graphic element by varying the font size of each line.

TIP: Use found objects to embellish your pages. Nia made a simple page accent from a label off a pair of jeans.

$ SOURCES Fonts: Impact (journaling), Zurich (title) off the Internet.

Rollin' Rollin' Rollin'   by Hilary Erickson

Circle-pattern paper mimics the action in Hilary's layout about her son Spencer's new rolling skills.

TIP: Create a clean design by grouping your elements into columns, as Hilary did with her photos and journaling.

$ SOURCES Patterned paper: American Crafts. Font: Times New Roman. Sticker: Pebbles In My Pocket.

Write your journaling in strips so you can easily position them in unique ways (or fix mistakes when needed).

Finding Your Voice by April Peterson

To tell the story of her son doubling his vocabulary in one day, April arranged her journaling strips so it would look like the words were coming out of his mouth.

TIP: Make a statement with a single photo enlarged to the length or width of the page. Many photo labs offer same-day service on prints larger than 8 × 10".

SOURCES Cardstock: Bazzill Basics Paper. Patterned paper: KI Memories. Font: Century Gothic. Chipboard letters, plastic letters, rub-ons: Heidi Swapp.

As with every new skill you've learned you must see the point in that skill before you embrace it. Talking has been no different. But a day spent with another boy your age, whose vocabulary is over 200 words, has made you see the point of talking.

I saw the way you looked when the other boy got what he wanted when he asked 'Milk?' Or how when he said 'Mama' he had his mommy's attention. Or after he said 'Train,' we went to take a closer look at it.

The next day you said door, drink, eat, oopps, dog, Mama- doubling your word count in a day. You saw the point, and you found your voice. I'm so glad to hear it.

FINDING Y•UR voice

Yum! by Jeannie van Wert

Jeannie chronicled her third child's first experience with solid foods with detailed info about his favorites and his hearty appetite.

TIP: Convert your photos to black-and-white using photo-editing software or at the photo lab so you can choose whatever paper colors you like.

SOURCES Cardstock, patterned paper, tacks: Chatterbox. Fonts: Vegetable Soup (title), Flea Market (journaling) by Two Peas in a Bucket. Rub-ons, floss: Making Memories.

Walker by April Peterson

April needed two pages to recount her son Xander's foray into walking. Her descriptive journaling and multiple action photos take the reader along for the ride.

TIP: Don't get hung up on grammar and punctuation when you write. Freeform journaling full of descriptive phrases can tell the story straight from the heart.

SOURCES Patterned paper: SEI (stripe), KI Memories (floral), Chatterbox (plaid). Vellum, acrylic flowers: KI Memories. Font: Teletype off the Internet. Ink: Tsukineko. Tags: Making Memories. Decorative-edge ruler: Plaid.

Hang a *calendar* in the baby's room. Every night, *jot down* tidbits from the day for future journaling.

Nikki Krueger, 2004 Creative Team member

Up-Downs!

September 2004

Think only football players do 'Up-Downs'?

Eight Month olds can, too!

They just don't get tired!

Or break a sweat from crawling to cruising!

Create an instant classic photo by converting your shot to black-and-white, or apply tints for a custom touch.

Up-Downs! by Tiffany Tillman

Using a football analogy and a couple quick lines of journaling, Tiffany described her baby's constant up-down movements at 8 months.

TIP: Show your baby's development by using pics of lots of stages. For example, if your baby is pulling herself up, capture the process in several photos.

SOURCES Software: Adobe Photoshop 7. Fonts: Tahoma (journaling), Aurora Cn BT (title) off the Internet. Digital elements: Designer Digitals (patterned paper), Shabby Princess (photo turn).

see the sketch

Smile, Grin, Laugh by Dana Smith

To capture her little girl's smile on film, Dana asked her sons to entertain their sister while she stood at the ready with her camera.

TIP: Let your title follow paths you create in your design. By arranging the sticker letters along the curved edge of her paper, Dana created a title that flows across the page.

SOURCES Patterned paper, stickers, chipboard accents: BasicGrey. Font: Age Old Love by Autumn Leaves. Epoxy accent: Autumn Leaves. Flowers: Prima. Rhinestones, rickrack: Making Memories.

Keep a *running list* on your computer of milestones or details of special *moments* as they happen.

Lisa Storms, 2006 Creative Team member

First Haircut by Rebecca Odom

Photos of her son's first haircut became a springboard for Rebecca to journal about how important she finds it to record all of his "firsts."

TIP: Layer small letters on top of large ones for an interesting title. Use a different letter style for each word so they're both easy to read.

SOURCES Patterned paper, stickers, punches, ribbon, rickrack: EK Success.

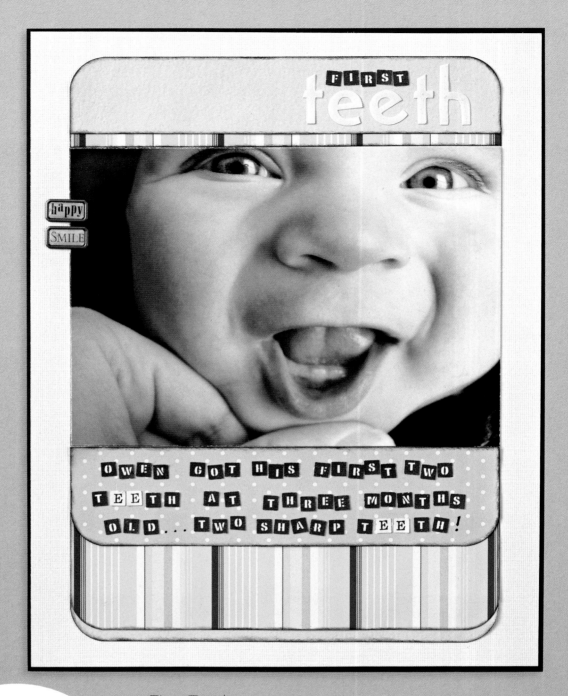

FIRST teeth

happy

SMILE

OWEN GOT HIS FIRST TWO TEETH AT THREE MONTHS OLD...TWO SHARP TEETH!

First Teeth by Lisa Storms

To go along with the tooth theme, Lisa gave the sticker letters in her title a glossy finish that mimics tooth enamel and used white letters for the e's in the word "teeth."

TIP: Incorporate symbolism into your layouts. Even if it's not immediately evident to the reader, it will subtly enhance the theme.

SOURCES Cardstock: Prism Papers. Patterned paper: Me and My Big Ideas (stripe). SEI (dot). Stickers: Arctic Frog. Stamps, punch: Stampin' Up!. Brads: K&Company.

Ink the edges of your paper to give them more definition on your page.

EATING FINGER FOOD

CLAPPING

SAYING DADA

BATH SEAT

PULLING UP

CRUISING

SHAKING HEAD NO

th DATES

7th month milestones

WAVING

FIRST FLU

TWO TEETH

7th-Month Milestones by Candi Gershon

Candi combined cute shots from a photo shoot with phrases about her daughter's new achievements.

TIP: If you don't have room for detailed journaling, hide it behind an element. Candi put the dates of her daughter's key milestones on the tag tucked behind the photos.

SOURCES Cardstock: Prism Papers. Patterned paper: Autumn Leaves. Font: Songwriter by Autumn Leaves. Stickers: Chatterbox. Stamps: PSX. Ink: Ranger Industries. Tags: 2Dye4. Buttons: SEI (small green, blue), Autumn Leaves (large green, yellow). Ribbon: Michael's.

Find a *place* where you can leave your supplies out all the time so you don't waste *time* searching for stuff.

Jen Lessinger, 2006 Creative Team member

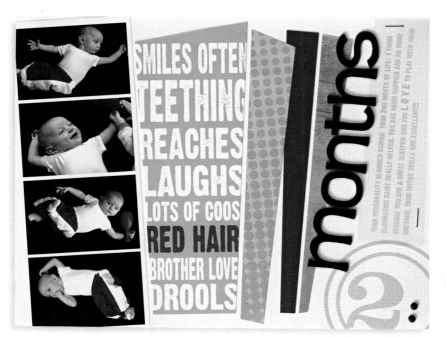

SMILES OFTEN
TEETHING
REACHES
LAUGHS
LOTS OF COOS
RED HAIR
BROTHER LOVE
DROOLS

months

2

2 Months by Erin Roe

Erin paired a group of photos printed as one long strip with irregularly cut strips of patterned paper for a playful look.

TIP: Repeat patterns, shapes, or colors on your page to help keep the eye moving. Erin used splashes of red to call attention to key areas.

$ **SOURCES** Patterned paper: SEI (green dots), BasicGrey (orange), Karen Foster Design (red). Fonts: Dirty Headline (journaling), Modern No. 20 (title) off the Internet. Chipboard letters: Scenic Route Paper Co.

timeline album

Erica Hernandez had already done traditional milestone layouts for her son Zachary as part of a larger album, and she wanted to have all his milestones in one place. She found a small accordion album she could use to create a compact timeline of Zachary's growth, keeping it simple with one photo and embellishment for each page.

1. Print a timeline of milestones and events on white cardstock. Erica printed each two-month spread on a single 9½ × 6½" piece of cardstock, alternating text colors for each. Glue the spreads to the album pages and add wide bands of cardstock in colors that match your text.

2. Select a favorite photo from each month, crop them all to the same size, and glue in place. Erica used a single sheet of stickers as accents for the album, using one phrase on each page.

3. Use rub-ons to place a title on the leathery surface of the album.

SOURCES Album: Target. Cardstock: Bazzill Basics Paper. Font: Century Gothic. Stickers: K&Company (phrases), Marcella by Kay for Target ("Zachary"). Rub-ons: Autumn Leaves (months), Die Cuts with a View (cover). Design: Erica Hernandez.

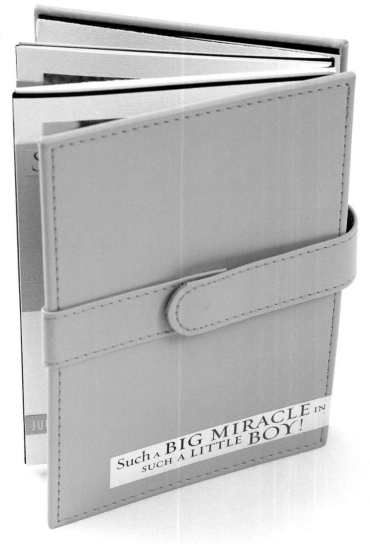

Such A BIG MIRACLE IN SUCH A LITTLE BOY!

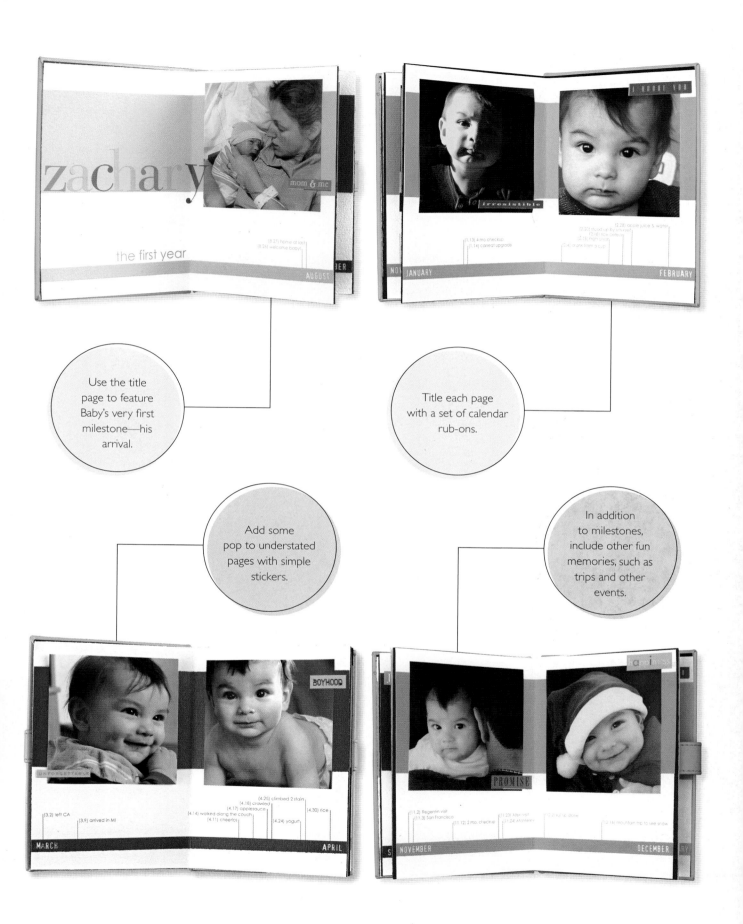

Use the title page to feature Baby's very first milestone—his arrival.

Title each page with a set of calendar rub-ons.

Add some pop to understated pages with simple stickers.

In addition to milestones, include other fun memories, such as trips and other events.

quick kit album

Mothers of toddlers, never fear: It's not too late to scrapbook baby photos. Erin Terrell found a quick and easy way to get a stack of baby photos of her daughter, Daisy, into a scrapbook—and Daisy is 8! With an album kit and cardstock, Erin saved time by not having to make several product choices, and she finished Daisy's album in a flash.

1. Start by choosing your photos. Because Erin's photos were of different scenes and had varying color schemes, she thought about scanning the prints and converting them all to black-and-white. But the coordinated and subtle pastel papers in the kit allowed her to mix photos with a variety of hues without severe color clashes.

2. Group your photos chronologically. Erin had a few years' worth of photos, so she decided to color-code the layouts. The pink layouts are from Daisy's first year, the purple from the next year, and so on.

3. Add simple embellishments. Using accents from a kit means you won't have to worry about finding matching pieces. The kit Erin used came with stickers, brads, ribbon, and decorative metal accents.

SOURCES Album kit: Making Memories. Design: Erin Terrell.

Mat all your photos with white cardstock for a cohesive look.

Find imaginative ways to use the kit's accents, such as the row and circle of brads here.

To fit many photos on a layout, reduce some to wallet-size and crop others.

Daily life

EATING, SLEEPING, AND playing—in everyday life, it's the simple things that make up a huge part of your baby's day. But don't write off those little moments just because they happen daily. In this chapter, we'll show off fun scrapbook pages that turn mundane activities into cherished memories.

see the sketch

Hanging Out by Erin Roe

Erin played up her "hanging out" theme by "hanging" photos and part of the title on this page about her family enjoying some quiet time.

TIP: Use accents to reinforce your theme. Erin fashioned a hanging sign out of a metal-rim tag and used two sizes of brads to convey the idea of hanging her photos.

SOURCES Patterned paper: Cactus Pink (green, stripe), Bo-Bunny Press (blue). Font: Baskerville Old Face off the Internet. Plastic accents, chipboard accents: Heidi Swapp. Brads: Autumn Leaves (large), Making Memories (small). Metal-rim tag: Making Memories. Embroidery floss: Michaels.

I woke up on a Saturday morning and found all 3 of my guys chillin' in the family room. Spencer was having a rough time with his teething and they were helping him through it. Blowing raspberries, giving him teethers and wiping up the drool.

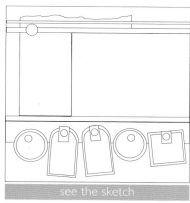

see the sketch

Sippy by Jennifer Bourgeault

A large photo and whimsical title adorn this ode to sippy cups, in which Jennifer recounts her family's attachment to the colorful kid cups.

TIP: Replace ribbons with strips of pretty paper. Jennifer threaded a thin strip of striped paper through a metal ribbon charm for classic style.

SOURCES Patterned paper, rivets, tags: Chatterbox. Font: Rust by Chatterbox. Stickers: Creative Imaginations ("S," script "P"), The Sticker Studio ("I"), Mrs. Grossman's (sans serif "P"), Me and My Big Ideas ("Y"). Ink: Ranger Industries. Ribbon charm, buttons, photo anchors, brads: Junkitz.

Do your layout in *segments*. Don't feel you have to finish it all at one time—an impossible task for a *mom* with a baby.

Leslie Lightfoot, 2005 Creative Team member

Laugh by Christy Palmer

Christy needed only a few words to express her feelings about this candid photo.

TIP: Get perfectly "printed" journaling without using your printer. Rub-on letters and phrases will give your page a polished look.

SOURCES Patterned paper: Junkitz. Rubber stamp: Hero Arts. Ink: Tsukineko ("laugh"), Stampin' Up! (stitch). Acrylic letters, rub-ons, ribbon: Heidi Swapp. Photo hangers, mini brads: Daisy D's Paper Co. Paper flower, button: Making Memories. Thread: Michaels.

No Wrong Way by Tiffany Tillman

Tiffany's baby, Carmelita, enjoyed the taste of spaghetti but loved covering herself in red sauce even more. Tiffany made the photo the main element on this digital page, then added color-coordinating circles for a clean design.

TIP: Skip journaling altogether if your title and photo say it all. Just add a date so you'll remember the timeline later.

SOURCES Software: Adobe Photoshop 7. Fonts: Avant Garde Md BT ("there's just," "to eat spaghetti!"), Aurora Cn BT ("no," "wrong way") off the Internet. Digital elements: Shabby Princess.

Carson's Favorite Things by Rebecca Cooper

Using snapshots taken at various times, Rebecca tracked her son's daily life on a page listing his favorite things.

TIP: "Print" white text on black paper by filling a text box in your word-processing software with a black background and changing your text color to white.

$ **SOURCES** Patterned paper, stickers: American Crafts. Font: Bookman off the Internet.

You can single handedly turn my house upside down in a matter of minutes. Since you started crawling, you've been out to explore every inch of your little world. I go around all day cleaning up and you follow right behind undoing all that I've just done!

You just love to pretend you're driving the car. You turn the wheel & giggle & grunt in that little manly way of yours. When the fun is over & it's Daddy's turn to drive you are not happy at all. We have to pry your little hands off the steering wheel.

You absolutely adore your big sister. You love to watch her playing and singing. In the morning when you first see Emily, your face just lights up. You follow her around the house all day and are starting to imitate the things that she does.

You know that family at church who always sits at the very back because they have such noisy kids! Well that's us. And the high pitched squeals coming from our bench are YOURS! You just love to hear the sound of your own voice noisy boy!

The vacuum is actually one of your NOT so favorite things. In fact you are downright terrified of it. When I bring out the vacuum you crawl away as fast as your little arms and legs will take you. Even when it is off I can't even get you to touch the thing.

Since you were a newborn you have been so fascinated with Buddy. I'm sad to say that the attraction is definitely not mutual. Buddy is quite scared of you. You've been known to pull hair and you get so excited whenever he's close to you that you hit him.

You are all about the finger food! You absolutely hate the mushy stuff. So the first finger food you tried was cheerios - and you loved them. It seems like I carry a container of cheerios with me everywhere we go now. What would we do without cheerios?

You are most definitely momma's little boy! Since the moment you were born it seems like you haven't ever *wanted* me to put you down. My favorite is when you snuggle up close, lay your head on my chest and play with my hair. I just love your sweet snuggles.

Carson's favorite things eight months old

I Love You by Anita Matejka

Anita wanted to remember the innocence of her napping five month old, so she got down to her baby's eye level and moved in close for a sweet shot that became the main element on her scrapbook page.

TIP: Wait until naptime to snap a photo—it's the perfect opportunity to easily catch a wonderful natural shot.

SOURCES Cardstock: American Crafts. Patterned paper: BasicGrey. Sticker: American Crafts. Acrylic accents: Heidi Swapp. Ink: Ranger Industries. Pen: Staedtler. Ribbon: KI Memories.

> When sorting photos, drop *pictures* you want to *scrapbook* into a page protector, along with any journaling or layout ideas, until you're *ready* to use them.
>
> Dana Smith, 2006 Creative Team member

M vs. K by Heather Melzer

Heather's daughters fight over every toy they own, but her littlest has started to stand up for herself. Heather designed a page inspired by a comic strip in order to play up the humor in the photos and journaling.

TIP: Take a page from the comics by using the structure of a panel as the map for your design. Strips of white paper mounted on adhesive foam make Heather's photos, journaling, and title look like part of a comic strip.

SOURCES Patterned paper, tab, sticker: SEI. Font: Century Gothic. Marker, metal letters: American Crafts. Foam backing: Artistic Expressions.

Swingin' by J.J. Killins

Pictures of J.J.'s daughter capture the pure joy and excitement of riding a swing for the first time, while the journaling expresses J.J.'s feelings about watching her baby grow up so fast.

TIP: Apply your own style to your embellishments with patterned paper, as J.J. did with the slide mounts that frame her smaller photos.

SOURCES Patterned paper: Paper Loft (wood grain), Daisy D's Paper Co. (circles), Autumn Leaves (floral). Fonts: Hootie (journaling), Emmascript (script journaling) off the Internet. Die cuts: DMD Industries. Stickers: Scrapworks. Ribbon: Hyman Hendler (dots), Offray (solid).

In Love with All of You by Shannon Brown

Shannon professed her love for all her baby's little parts in this layout that puts the focus on the photos. The large photo becomes a backdrop for smaller shots raised with adhesive foam.

TIP: When stretching a photo across two pages, make sure the split doesn't fall in an important place, like the subject's face.

SOURCES Patterned paper: KI Memories. Stickers: Wordsworth ("in love with," "of"), Mrs. Grossman's ("all," "you"). Stamps: Hero Arts. Ink: Tsukineko. Pen: EK Success. Buttons: Making Memories.

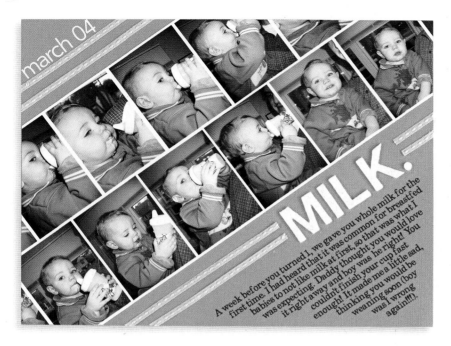

march 04

MILK.

A week before you turned 1, we gave you whole milk for the first time. I had heard that it was common for breastfed babies to not like milk at first, so that was what I was expecting. Daddy thought you would love it right away and boy was he right! You couldn't finish your cup fast enough! It made me a little sad, thinking you would be weaning soon (boy was I wrong again!!!).

Milk by Erin Roe

Erin got lots of cute photos of her son's first taste of whole milk. To spice up a neutral background, she mimicked the stripes in Bryce's shirt with ribbon.

TIP: Align multiple images from a photo shoot at an angle to give a simple page a jolt of energy.

SOURCES Cardstock: Bazzill Basics Paper. Font: Sandra Oh (journaling) off the Internet. Felt stickers: CPE Enterprises. ("milk"). Rub-ons: Making Memories ("march 04"). Ribbon: May Arts.

GET ORGANIZED

Photos tend to pile up when you live with a new baby. So many photoworthy moments, so little time to keep them organized. Follow these quick steps to get that pile under control.

1. Gather up all your photos so you can see how much you have to organize.

2. Decide on a system. There's no right or wrong way to categorize your photos. You can do it by date or event. With a new baby, a chronological approach is often the easiest and will help when it comes to documenting your baby's growth.

3. Get sorting. Set up a temporary space, such as a large table, where you can spread out. Have several boxes or bins on hand to use as temporary storage, and use a sticky note to label each container with the categories you've identified. Tackle this task in short spurts here and there, such as those 15 minutes when your little one actually falls asleep.

4. Write the essential facts—date, occasion, and so on—on the backs of your photos. Remember to use photo-safe, quick-drying pens to record the information, or use a sticky note to prevent damaging the print.

5. Once everything is labeled, place your photos in photo file boxes or photo albums. Make sure your system is archival, and store it in the right environment—places that do not have extreme fluctuations in temperature (especially heat), high humidity, or direct sunlight.

6. Once you've caught up on your little one's photos, you can keep your system going by labeling photos as they come in. Be careful about storing your photos in photo lab envelopes—they aren't always safe for long-term storage. You can find archival envelopes at scrapbook stores or online.

Machine-sewn
or hand-stitched
detailing adds loads
of texture and polish.
Short on time? Fake the
look with rub-ons
or stamps.

The Way You Play by Amy Howe

Amy's daughter and baby boy made up a goofy game that they love to play—
a simple sequence Amy captured in her snapshots and journaling.

TIP: Document interactions between your children. Good or bad, the quirks in their
relationships are worth preserving.

SOURCES Cardstock: Bazzill Basics Paper. Patterned paper, photo turn: BasicGrey. Font:
Typoslabserif Light off the Internet. Ink: Tsukineko. Acrylic paint: Folk Art from Plaid. Pen: American
Crafts. Plastic accents: Heidi Swapp. Chipboard accents: Heidi Swapp ("way," "play"), BasicGrey
(flowers). Tacks: Chatterbox. Thread: Coats and Clark.

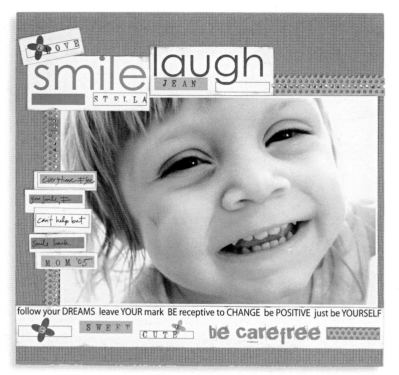

follow your DREAMS leave YOUR mark BE receptive to CHANGE be POSITIVE just be YOURSELF

SWEET   CUTE   be carefree

Smile Laugh by Alecia Grimm

All Alecia needed to create this quick page about her daughter was an adorable photo and a few preprinted phrases cut from a sheet of patterned paper.

TIP: Don't overthink it. Enlarge your favorite photo and add some phrase stickers and a few key descriptors for a really quick page that will make you smile.

SOURCES Cardstock: Die Cuts with a View. Patterned paper: Urban Lily. Mesh: Magic Mesh. Rubber stamp: Provo Craft. Ink: Clearsnap. Rhinestones: Westrim Crafts. Pen: EK Success.

While your baby is napping some afternoon, *sort* your patterned *paper* by color or theme for *quicker* picks later.

Erin Roe, 2006 Creative Team member

Payton Isabella by Talia Audenart

Capture the essence of a season in a snapshot of your baby enjoying it. Talia surrounded a single photo with handwritten journaling strips and added colors and accents that remind her of fall.

TIP: Accentuate your baby's small size by taking a picture from above.

SOURCES Cardstock: Bazzill Basics Paper. Patterned paper: KI Memories (brown floral), Making Memories (ledger), Provo Craft (yellow floral). Rub-on: KI Memories. Ink: Clearsnap. Pen: Signo from Sanford. Brads: American Crafts. Flower: Jo-Ann Stores. Ribbon: Heidi Swapp (dot, pink, light brown), Making Memories (brown).

Scan maps or newspaper clippings into your computer and print them on cardstock for archival-safe custom backgrounds.

TV Eyes by Heather Melzer

A photo of Heather's baby girl, Katie, with her big sister and the family dog—enthralled by a TV show—is the focal point for a page about Katie's favorite shows.

TIP: Rethink existing supplies. Heather turned a little wood frame into a TV-inspired accent with a few twists of wire.

SOURCES Patterned paper, wood frame: Chatterbox. Font: Century Gothic (journaling). Marker: American Crafts. Flower: Imagination Project. Photo corners: Heidi Swapp. Paper clip: Junkitz. Rhinestone: Westrim Crafts. Wire: Jo-Ann Stores.

Things I Love About You by Nasilele Holland

A simple photo and a background filled with journaling enabled Nasilele to capture her favorite everyday memories of her daughter as a baby.

TIP: Remember to repeat phrases when filling your background with journaling you want people to read, since some of it will be obscured by the photo.

$ SOURCES Cardstock: Bazzill Basics Paper. Patterned paper: Rusty Pickle. Font: American Typewriter off the Internet. Stickers: American Crafts. Ribbon: Lin's Trimmings.

Life in Diapers by Tracy Odachowski

Tracy snapped pics of her daughter's daily activities and jotted down questions she would love for her baby to be able to answer.

TIP: Infuse your pages with your baby's perspective by taking photos from her point of view.

SOURCES Cardstock: Bazzill Basics Paper. Patterned paper, clips: Scrapworks. Font: Abadi Mt Condensed off the Internet. Stickers: Chatterbox ("life"), Scrapworks ("diapers"). Rub-ons: Making Memories. Ribbon: Stampin' Up!.

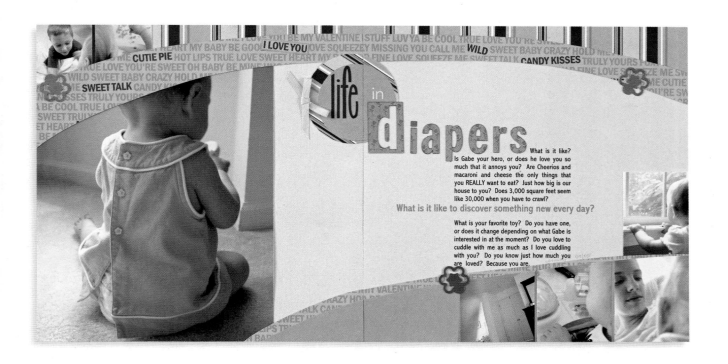

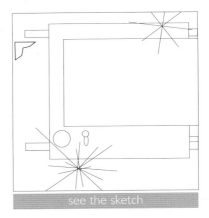

see the sketch

Sleeping Baby by Leah Zion

Leah made a large photo of her son sleeping the focus for this page about her son's transition from baby to toddler.

TIP: Photograph your baby sleeping. Jot down your thoughts and feelings about your child at that very moment to include later as journaling.

SOURCES Cardstock: Bazzill Basics Paper (dark red), Arctic Frog (brown). Patterned paper, stickers: Arctic Frog. Font: Powderfinger Type off the Internet. Rub-ons: Arctic Frog ("baby," brackets), Autumn Leaves (stitch), KI Memories (heart). Photo turns: 7Gypsies. Chipboard accent: Li'l Davis Designs. Rhinestone, pearl: Making Memories. Ribbon: American Crafts. Punch: EK Success.

In 5 minutes, you will wake up.

You will rub your eyes, smile, climb off the bed, and run down the hallway calling for your Papa. You will transform into a loud, playful, sweet little boy. But right now, I will cherish this moment where I see less of a toddler, and more of my quickly disappearing

Sleeping {Baby}

Aah... What a busy day! I had to eat 5 whole meals. And that's not including Johnny's, which I finished for him. Along with watching a movie or two and emptying out all of the silverware and measuring cups from the drawers, I managed to digest 3 crayons and a marble. Time to Relax.

Taking life **Easy**

Taking Life Easy by Bethany Laakkonen

According to Bethany, her little brother lives an easy life yet kicks back in his little red "throne" as though exhausted from his daily activities.

TIP: Create bold accents simply by cutting shapes out of paper. On this digital layout, Bethany "cut" small and large circles of digital patterns to form an eye-catching border.

SOURCES Software: Adobe Photoshop 2. Fonts: Jane Austen ("taking life"), Impact ("Easy") off the Internet, Times New Roman (journaling). Digital elements: Shabby Princess (patterned paper, scratched overlay, stitching), Spaceraven (brushes). Photo: Sharon Laakkonen.

THINKING "WRITE"

As a parent of a little one, you have minimal time to dedicate to scrapbooking. And when the opportunity presents itself, journaling can sometimes slow you down, especially when you're trying to dredge up details about a particular photo. Use these tips to make journaling a speedy and painless process.

- **Jot it down.** Keep a notepad and pen on hand to write down cute things your child does or milestone moments as they happen. Tuck a pad in your purse, glove compartment, and next to your bed so you're prepared wherever inspiration strikes.

- **Think digitally.** Use e-mails and blogs (Web logs) to keep relatives and friends in the loop. Then print copies of the entries or messages for your scrapbook. You can cut, paste, and save them in a word-processing document, then format and print when you're ready to scrap.

- **Keep paperwork.** Day care and doctor reports can be great sources of info. Daily or weekly caregiver reports about activities or doctor's notes about your baby's growth are great summaries of his life.

- **Let others speak.** At a loss for words? There's a good chance that a poem or quote can help you. Children's books, dictionaries, and scrapbook Web sites are just a few places you'll find poems and quotes for your pages. And you can pick up scrapbook supplies with printed quotes and phrases for all sorts of subjects.

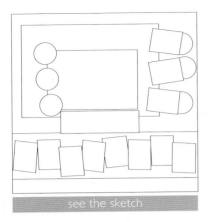

see the sketch

Your Tiny Little Teeth by Vicky Gibson

Vicky thought her son Kaya looked so cute brushing his new little teeth, she couldn't stop taking photos of him. It was too hard to choose just one when it came time to do the layout, so she included them all by printing several of them small.

TIP: Track on small details. Vicky charted the order in which her son's teeth arrived and jotted down the sequence along the left and top edges of the page.

SOURCES Cardstock: Bazzill Basics Paper. Patterned paper: BasicGrey. Rub-ons, acrylic letters: KI Memories. Foam stamps: Making Memories. Ink: Tsukineko (white), Making Memories (sepia). Pen: Sakura of America.

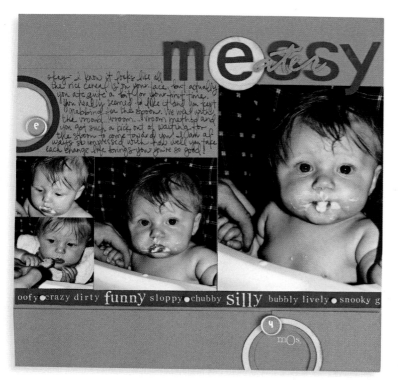

Messy Eater by Kara Jones

Kara's page is a record of the first time her daughter ate solid food—a successful but messy endeavor.

TIP: Design a custom page title by printing words or letters in reverse on cardstock and cutting out the pieces with sharp scissors or a craft knife.

SOURCES Cardstock: Bazzill Basics Paper (orange, yellow, green), WorldWin (brown). Fonts: OCRB ("messy"), Rage Italic ("eater") off the Internet. Stickers: EK Success. Rub-ons: Chatterbox. Ink: Fiber Scraps. Pen: Sanford. Brads: Karen Foster Design. Metal tags, circle cutter: EK Success.

Great Lash Moment by Nicole Gartland

When Nicole discovered her daughter, Natalie, playing with mascara, she just laughed and took pictures for this satirical spread about a girl growing up.

TIP: Let your subject's gaze guide you and place photos so the person is looking into the page or at other objects, as Nicole did with her top image.

SOURCES Patterned paper: KI Memories (black), Karen Foster Design (green). Fonts: Sleigh Ride (title), Blueberry Pie (journaling) by Two Peas in a Bucket. Die cut: KI Memories.

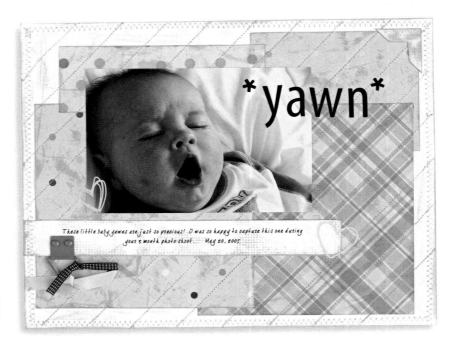

Yawn   by Emily Dennis

Emily caught this sweet yawn during her son's three-month photo shoot.

TIP: Give different patterned papers a similar look by skimming them with an ink pad.

SOURCES Cardstock: Bazzill Basics Paper. Patterned paper: Chatterbox (plaid, yellow polka dot), KI Memories (blue). Font: Dear Joe off the Internet. Stickers: Doodlebug Design. Rub-ons: KI Memories. Ink: Ranger Industries. Ribbon: Offray. Photo hanger: Daisy D's Paper Co.

When you buy an album, get *refill* pages and inserts *right away* so you won't have to hunt for them later.

Leah Fung, contributing editor

Favorite Blanket   by Dana Smith

Dana attached a corner of her son's well-loved blanket to this page for a sure-to-be-treasured keepsake.

TIP: Attach actual baby items to your layouts by machine-stitching fabrics right to the background.

SOURCES Cardstock: Prism Papers. Patterned paper: BasicGrey. Font: Cleanliness by Autumn Leaves. Fibers, tag, letter stickers: BasicGrey. Rub-ons: Making Memories. Jump ring: Junkitz. Brads: SEI. Chipboard accents: BasicGrey (heart), Heidi Swapp ("blanket").

Experts say a nursing woman needs about 500 extra calories a day. Hmmm, I question the 500; I think it's probably more like, 5,000? You see, in the first few months after your birth, I was constantly hungry. I would eat a full meal and have dessert, then an hour later, I find myself hungry again. Well, preparing meals every hour while taking care of a newborn and a 3-year-old is out of the question. I needed quick and easy foods. So, I turned to ice cream! Actually, I CRAVED ice cream! Probably because I'm not a milk drinker, and I needed the extra calcium. I finished a gallon of Breyer's Cookies and Cream ice cream every couple of days! Daddy once commented that my habit was getting expensive. My reply was, "It's still cheaper than buying formula!" Actually, that might not have been true, though it sounded good at the time! You didn't end up too, too chubby, but when people commented on your fatties, I told them, "Oh yeah, she's got Body by Breyer's!"

Body by Breyer's   by Nely Fok

A picture of Nely's cute, chubby baby and a colorful letter-sticker title were the perfect combo for a playful page about Nely's post-pregnancy ice-cream cravings.

TIP: Pick a photo of your baby as the visual for your favorite parenting and nursing stories. Layouts with baby pictures don't have to be just about the baby.

SOURCES Patterned paper, stickers: Urban Lily. Fonts: House Slant ("body by") by House Industries, American Typewriter (journaling) off the Internet. Die cuts: Scrapworks. Ink: Clearsnap. Flowers: Sarah Heidt Photo Craft.

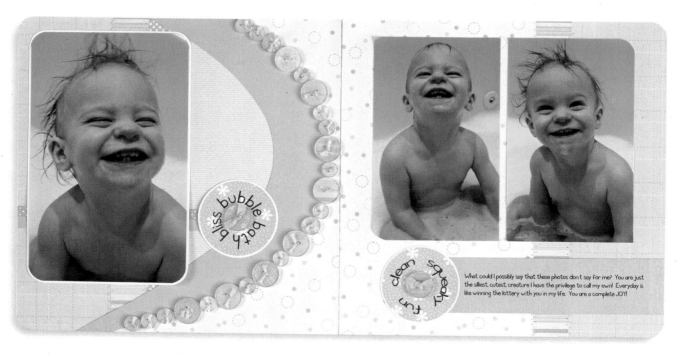

Bubble Bath Bliss   by Cindy Smith

The curved lines and rounded corners give a slightly retro vibe to this spread about Cindy's baby enjoying a bath.

TIP: Make matching accents with papers a snap by backing clear buttons with patterned paper that coordinates with your layout.

SOURCES Cardstock: Bazzill Basics Paper. Patterned paper: Sweetwater. Font: Cleanliness by Autumn Leaves. Ribbon: Offray. Buttons: Autumn Leaves. Thread: DMC.

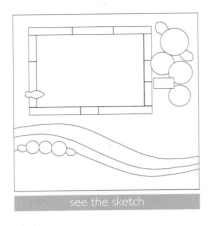

see the sketch

Delight by Valerie Salmon

Valerie used a set of matched supplies from one manufacturer to pull together this page featuring a favorite photo of her little girl.

TIP: Look for items and colors in your photos that can direct your paper and accent choices. Valerie was inspired by the lively pink hat with layered flowers in this picture.

SOURCES Cardstock: Bazzill Basics Paper. Patterned paper, rub-ons, stickers, woven labels, tags, photo turn: K&Company. Chipboard accent: Li'l Davis Designs. Paper flowers, pink brad: Making Memories. Ribbon: May Arts.

{STRETCH}

and

Snooze

Little Brinley. One week old.

Stretch and Snooze by Amy Farnsworth

Amy was lucky to catch her newborn daughter stretching and falling back to sleep, so she used all seven photos.

TIP: When using lots of photos, make one the focal point, as Amy did, by enlarging it and placing it on different paper.

SOURCES Patterned paper: Chatterbox. Fonts: Cadence ("snooze") by Autumn Leaves, Bank Gothic ("stretch"), Century Gothic ("and," journaling) off the Internet. Ink: Ranger Industries. Flower, ribbon, safety pin: Making Memories.

Use your own *handwriting.* It's quicker than computer printing, and it will be *special* to your child in the future.

Rhonda Bonifay, 2006 Creative Team member

In a single moment of insanity, Abby decides that the roll of toilet paper is much better all unrolled and in the toilet. "AH-WET!" she declares. Ah yes. It's all wet. And you need to get out of the toilet. And I need to remember to keep the door shut.

get out

of the toilet

Get Out of the Toilet by Nic Howard

When her daughter, Abby, crawled into the bathroom and filled the toilet with toilet paper, Nic grabbed the camera to capture the moment for this colorful page.

TIP: Punch holes in your background to form a concentric circular design that leads the eye across the page toward your main photo.

SOURCES Cardstock: Bazzill Basics Paper. Patterned paper: Scenic Route Paper Co. Fonts: Scratchy Toad (title) by Two Peas in a Bucket, Century Gothic (journaling). Hole punch: Making Memories.

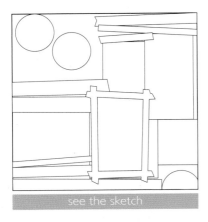

see the sketch

Payton Lou-Who by Talia Audenart

Four photos of Talia's daughter Payton looking like one of Dr. Seuss's "Whos" with her sproutlike ponytail grace this playful pieced-together page.

TIP: Frame a favorite photo on your layout with four strands of ribbon and colorful brads in the corners.

SOURCES Cardstock: Bazzill Basics Paper. Patterned paper: American Crafts (dots), KI Memories (light green floral, white floral, purple floral). Pen, brads, ribbon: American Crafts. Decorative tape, foam stamp: Heidi Swapp. Staples: Office Depot.

May 20 by Jen Lessinger

For Jen, giving her son Griffin his first bottle signified the end of her maternity leave, so she stood by with camera in hand while her older son took on the task.

TIP: Use a date as your title. By focusing on the date, Jen made a standard occasion all the more memorable.

 SOURCES Cardstock: Die Cuts with a View (teal), National Cardstock (kraft), DMD Industries (white). Patterned paper: Magic Scraps. Font: Don't Walk Run off the Internet. Stickers, marker: American Crafts. Chipboard accents: Heidi Swapp. Wood frame, tag: Chatterbox. Acrylic paint: Making Memories. File clip: Office Depot.

Ask *family members* to help out with journaling by writing their thoughts and *feelings* about the baby.

Nia Reddy, 2006 Creative Team member

Tubby by Brittany Laakkonen

Brittany loves her brother's tubby legs, seen here in a large photo with machine-stitched edges and journaling around its corner.

TIP: Make a custom title by covering chipboard letters with patterned paper or acrylic paint.

SOURCES Cardstock: Bazzill Basics Paper. Patterned paper: Arctic Frog. Ink: Clearsnap. Pen: Zig Writer by EK Success. Paint, brad, chipboard accents: Making Memories.

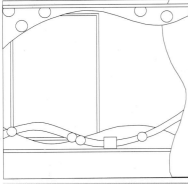

see the sketch

Clap Clap Clap by Jennifer Bourgeault

A simple photo of her daughter clapping gave Jennifer a great opportunity to create a page about her daughter's happiness.

TIP: To get more mileage out of your chipboard letters, also use the negative space, which shows the letter as a cutout.

SOURCES Textured paper: Provo Craft. Fonts: Proud Papa (quote) by Two Peas in a Bucket, Marita (script). Chipboard accents: Li'l Davis Designs (polka dot), Heidi Swapp (black). Epoxy sticker: Junkitz. Flowers: Prima (green), Doodlebug Design (pink, black). Ink: Clearsnap. Acrylic paint: Making Memories.

"If you're happy and you know it, clap your hands."

Well, if clapping is truly an indication of being happy, then you must be the happiest baby girl around! You first learned to clap your hands at ten months old, and I swear you haven't stopped since. Your most favorite time to clap is when you are watching Barney or the Wiggles on television. And, of course, whenever you do something that you are proud of...YAY, Lily! Just keep on clapping, baby girl, and we'll keep on clapping with you!

I Love to Eat   by Brittany Laakkonen

Brittany surrounded a photo of her brother, Josiah, enjoying a snack with vintage-looking patterned paper layered on black cardstock.

TIP: Write a white title and journaling on a dark background for extra impact. Brittany placed white letter stickers on brown patterned paper and cut around the letters so it looked as if someone had taken bites out of the title.

SOURCES Cardstock: Prism Papers. Patterned paper: Creative Imaginations (gold), 7Gypsies (brown), Rusty Pickle (bottle caps), Marcella by Kay (heart). Stickers: Mustard Moon ("eat"), Doodlebug Design ("I," "to"). Die cuts: Melissa Frances. Pen: Sharpie. Rub-ons: Making Memories. Brad: Queen & Co.

> Stock up on *cardstock* and patterned paper that *match* your baby's wardrobe so you'll always have supplies *on hand.*
>
> Lisa Storms, 2006 Creative Team member

Sweet Love   by Amy Martin

To showcase a favorite photo, Amy pieced together a heart from patterned-paper scraps in this digital layout. The curved journaling on the left becomes a decorative element itself.

TIP: Mimic Amy's digital effects with traditional materials, such as rub-on stitches and letter stickers on photos.

SOURCES Software: Corel PaintShop Pro. Patterned paper: Scrapartist. Fonts: Jjstencil ("Love"), Justy I ("sweet"), Pushkin (journaling) off the Internet. Digital elements: Scrapbook Elements. Photo: Joyce Godbold.

Create your own patterned paper by dressing up plain stock with rubber-stamped designs in any color.

1st Report by Heather Melzer

Heather documented her pride over the progress reports she received from her daughter's day care teachers in this page that includes a place to store and display the reports they wrote.

TIP: Construct a large pocket on your scrapbook page for storing memorabilia. Print your journaling on cardstock, cut out a pocket shape, and attach it to your layout by applying adhesive only along the outside edges.

SOURCES Cardstock: Prism Papers. Patterned paper, stickers: Sandylion. Font: MBell off the Internet. Rubber stamp: Hero Arts. Ink: Stampin' Up!. Marker: American Crafts.

Kate Melzer

Date of Birth: 11/04/05
Date: 5/05/05

Kate is a delightful little girl. She has become a very important part of classroom in a very short time. She is such fun. All the children a enjoy our friendship with Kate.

Physical and Gross Motor Development
Kate is sitting independently without support. She is ab postural security after leaning forward or trying to re the time! She does not like to "fall" out of this posi chest and upper body off the floor when placed tummy to back, side to side, changes directi movement. Kate is a strong infant with go a lot of the time and is becoming co materials or other children. She like with good strength and control for

Fine Motor Developmen
Kate is reaching, grasping hand to mouth. She is s offered a drink. She in coordination. She transfer. She is

Commun
Kate has
eve
Sh
c

Every six months or so, we go to the girls' school and visit with their teachers to get a progress report on how they're doing in the hours that they are away from us. It's always so much fun to hear about what they're eating, how they're napping and the fun things they like to do during at school. Katie's six month report was very positive. Miss Margaret told us how much they enjoy having her in class, how much fun she is, and how she is a great eater. It was also fun to hear the similarities and differences between Katie and her big sister, since Miss Margaret starting caring for both of them at eight weeks of age. It means so much to us to hear how much her teachers care for her. We left the meeting feeling so proud of her and all she has accomplished.

1st rePort

Walker by Valerie Salmon

To match the vibrancy of these photos of her son playing in his favorite walker, Valerie wrapped them in bands of colorful paper.

TIP: Make smaller photos stand out on a large page by giving them special matting treatments like the layered and curved ones on this page.

SOURCES Cardstock: Bazzill Basics Paper. Patterned paper: KI Memories. Font: Highlight (journaling) by Autumn Leaves, Geeza Pro ("little"), Baskerville ("Ian's") off the Internet. Stickers: Doodlebug Design. Chipboard accent: Pressed Petals. Large decorative brads: K&Company. Felt fabric: Jo-Ann Stores.

Use your trusty *punches* (such as a large square) to get a quick, *uniform* look on photos and paper.

Erin Roe, 2006 Creative Team member

I Love That Face by Kelly Goree

Several snapshots of her son's face are the perfect accompaniment to Kelly's journaling about the looks she loves to see.

TIP: To balance a large focal photo, cluster several smaller photos next to it. Add a thin, contrasting mat to your second favorite photo to make it pop and bring in color from other parts of the page.

 SOURCES Patterned paper: Chatterbox (plaid), Frances Meyer (car), FiberMark (green embossed, linen texture). Stickers: Mrs. Grossman's. Die cuts: Scrapworks. Rub-ons: Déjà Views for The C-Thru Ruler Company. Chipboard letters: Heidi Swapp. Ink: Clearsnap. Woven label: Making Memories.

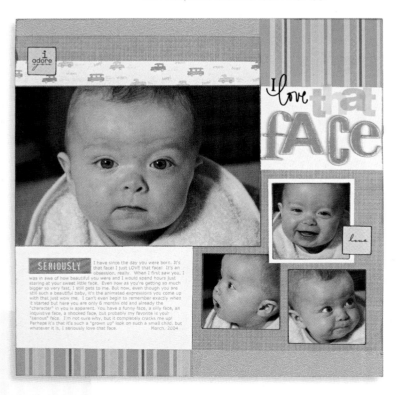

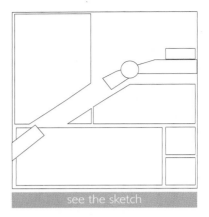

see the sketch

A Love for Shoes by Tracey Odachowski

Tracey wanted to document her daughter's quirky love of shoes, so she coupled detail shots of her little girl's shoe collection and feet with photos of her playing with them.

TIP: Give your photos a worn look by sanding the edges with a sanding block or distressing tool.

SOURCES Patterned paper: BasicGrey. Sticker, metal letters: Making Memories. Chipboard letters: Heidi Swapp. Rub-ons: Chatterbox. Pens: Stampin' Up!. Clip: The Card Connection for Michaels. Ribbon: Les Bon Ribbon. Nailhead: unknown.

smit·ten

a love for SHOES

IT CAN TAKE A LIFETIME TO TRULY APPRECIATE SHOES.

That's how it was for me. It took all nine months of my life to discover the love. Sure, my mother was trying to encourage it before then - she'd buy any girly shoe she saw to get me to notice them. Bunny slippers. Black patent leather. Sneakers. Even shimmery snow boots that I can't even fit into yet. They were all there waiting to be discovered.

So, what took me so long? I wish I knew. But, one day, I looked down at my feet, and there they were. Sweet, beautiful shoes. Staring back at me. Love at first sight - it just took me a while to see them, I guess. I love how they wrap around my feet. I love how my toes peek through the tops of my sandals. I love the way they complete an outfit.

BUT, WHAT DO I LOVE THE MOST ABOUT SHOES? the taste

Bubble Baby by Heather Melzer

Using a large photo of her daughter Katie and circle accents that look like bubbles floating across the page, Heather created a digital layout about seeing her baby wrapped in bubbles.

TIP: Digital designs don't have to stay that way. You can easily translate computer-made layouts like this one into paper designs using stickers or rub-ons, scraps of patterned papers, and ribbon.

SOURCES Software: Microsoft Digital Image Pro. Digital elements: Digital Design Essentials. Font: Swiss 721 Thin (journaling) off the Internet.

Buy a *kit* full of coordinated baby paper and accents, and save time by not having to *match* everything.

Helen Naylor, 2004 Creative Team member

Ella by Lori Thompson

While playing with her daughter one day, Lori caught this sweet photo of her with dimples and drool—the perfect companion to a list of family nicknames.

TIP: If you find you don't have enough stickers to spell your title, improvise. Lori cut off the arms of a "K" to get an extra "L."

SOURCES Cardstock: Bazzill Basics Paper. Patterned paper: Anna Griffin (paisley, stripe), Chatterbox (flower). Fonts: Frazzled ("girlie girl"), Typo ("sweet pea"), Wrought Iron ("smellie ellie") by Two Peas in a Bucket; MA Sexy ("droolie girl"), Curly Coryphaeus ("ellie bellie"), Tweed ("punky doodle") off the Internet. Stickers, flowers: Making Memories. Ink: Ranger Industries. Brads: Making Memories (pink), Jo-Ann Stores (pewter).

Dance Like No One Is Watching

by Heather Melzer

At the center of this digital page is one of Heather's favorite pictures of her daughter Katie dancing with reckless abandon.

TIP: Arrange a few page elements off-kilter—like the photo and paper background on this page—to mirror an energetic subject.

SOURCES Software: Microsoft Digital Image Pro. Fonts: Fragile (title) by Two Peas in a Bucket, Bodoni DTC (quote marks) off the Internet, Flighty (journaling) by Autumn Leaves. Digital elements: Designer Digitals (patterned paper, stitching, flower, inked edge), Two Peas in a Bucket (brush).

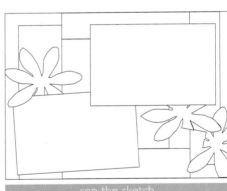

see the sketch

Stroller Baby

by Nicole Gartland

Nicole's daughter, Naomi, spends a lot of time in her stroller, so naturally Nicole had lots of photos of her in it. She featured her favorites in this patchwork-style page.

TIP: To make elements like this page's sticker-letter title and cut-out flowers stand out against a busy background, outline them with a pen or stamping ink.

SOURCES Patterned paper, stickers: Scenic Route Paper Co. Ink: Stewart Superior Corp.

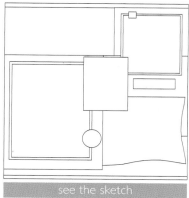

see the sketch

Binky

by Leah Fung

Leah's baby, Andrew, loved his pacifier but often lost it. Her journaling records one of those frantic searches and his brother's teasing.

TIP: Instead of printing your text in a special shape, easily add interest by trimming your text box creatively.

SOURCES Cardstock, patterned paper, die cut, tag, photo corners: Chatterbox. Font: Times New Roman. Chipboard accents: Pressed Petals. Metal accents: K&Company (tag), Artchix Studio (hardware). Ribbon: American Crafts.

Buy frequently used *supplies,* such as adhesive and cardstock, in bulk or *stock up* when they go on sale.

Leah Fung, contributing editor

Playmates Forever

by Jlyne Hanback

Jlyne loved this black-and-white photograph of her kids playing together, so she centered the matted photo atop an array of patterned-paper strips and placed a hand-cut heart around their faces.

TIP: If you have a photograph that you don't want to crop, use a frame to draw the eye to the subject.

SOURCES Patterned paper, photo corner: Chatterbox. Font: Avant Garde (journaling), P22 DaVinci (title) off the Internet. Rub-ons: Imagination Project (flowers), Making Memories ("forever").

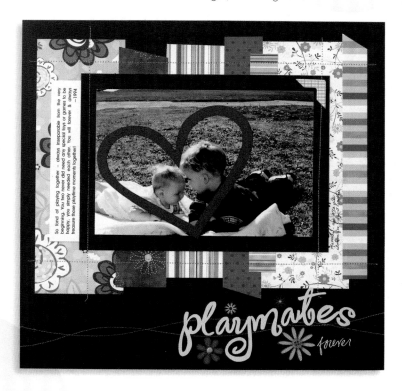

Carrots by Nicole Gartland

Nicole's daughter, Naomi, loved only one baby food—carrots. So this fun layout features two large carrots made from bands of patterned paper.

TIP: Put your stash of scrap paper to work by punching paper accents or piecing together a playful design that takes center stage on your page.

SOURCES Cardstock, patterned paper: Chatterbox. Stickers: Scenic Route Paper Co. ("a"), SEI (all other). Ink: Stampin' Up!. Punch: Marvy Uchida (circle), EK Success (asterisk).

Define the edges of your paper pieces by inking them. The outline gives your page a 3-D look without adding bulk.

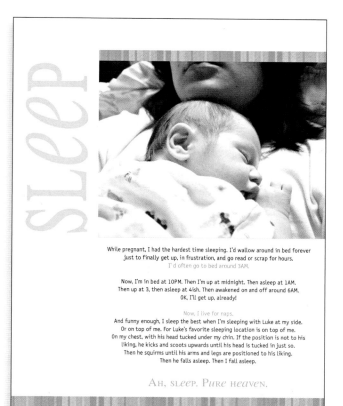

While pregnant, I had the hardest time sleeping. I'd wallow around in bed forever just to finally get up, in frustration, and go read or scrap for hours.
I'd often go to bed around 3AM.

Now, I'm in bed at 10PM. Then I'm up at midnight. Then asleep at 1AM. Then up at 3, then asleep at 4ish. Then awakened on and off around 6AM. OK, I'll get up, already!

Now, I live for naps.
And funny enough, I sleep the best when I'm sleeping with Luke at my side. Or on top of me. For Luke's favorite sleeping location is on top of me. On my chest, with his head tucked under my chin. If the position is not to his liking, he kicks and scoots upwards until his head is tucked in just so. Then he squirms until his arms and legs are positioned to his liking. Then he falls asleep. Then I fall asleep.

AH, SLEEP. PURE HEAVEN.

Sleep by Linda Barber

Linda crafted a simple ode to sleep in this streamlined digital design that includes info on her son's sleep patterns and the joy she feels when her son falls asleep in her arms.

TIP: Crop for impact. In the image Linda used on this page, she put the focus on Baby while keeping a hint of herself in the shot for context.

SOURCES Software: Adobe Photoshop CS2. Fonts: Will&Grace (title), Saturday Sans (journaling) off the Internet. Digital elements: ScrapKitchen (patterned paper).

> Take your *photos* with you to the store when you buy supplies so you don't *waste* time (and money) *buying* paper that won't work with your pictures.
>
> Candi Gershon, contributing editor

While still pregnant, Grandma Julie showed me the beautiful bracelet she bought for you. As adorable as it was, I was certain that it was going to be too small. After all, I already had a baby before and he couldn't have possibly ever been that small. Well how soon we forget. The tiny bracelet fit your wrist perfectly, Lillian. So small. So beautiful. So perfect.

Tiny Bracelet by Jennifer Bourgeault

Jennifer used a delicate bracelet on her page to creatively show just how tiny her newborn daughter was.

TIP: Find a way to include keepsakes on your page. If you don't want to permanently adhere your little treasure, try attaching it with ribbon or trim, as Jennifer did.

SOURCES Patterned paper, vellum: Paper Adventures. Font: Heber by Chatterbox. Stickers: All My Memories. Acrylic accents: Creative Imaginations.

daily life album

Knowing that her son won't remember his daily routines when he grows up, Erin Roe captured the memories for him with a day-in-the-life album that chronicles his earliest adventures.

1. Create a standard template you can use with each page. Erin divided her page into quadrants that gave her the versatility to put photos, journaling, and patterned papers in different blocks on each page without having to come up with new dimensions each time.

2. Cut coordinating patterned papers, your photos, and your journaling into squares. In Erin's case, each of her elements needed to be a 4" square to fit in every quadrant.

3. Vary the placement of your elements to keep the design interesting, and keep it unified by choosing just a single accent style to be used throughout the book.

SOURCES Album, woven letters: Making Memories. Patterned paper: KI Memories (stripe, circles), BasicGrey (blue). Fonts: Georgia (serif), Charisma (script) by Autumn Leaves, Oh Baby! (dingbats) by David Walker. Stickers: BasicGrey. Wood accents: BasicGrey. Design: Erin Roe.

A BABY'S life

Use a sweet detail shot of your baby's little feet or hands for the title page.

coming
HOME

The day after you were born we brought you home from the hospital. I couldn't wait for you to start your life at home with the whole family together. I snapped some pictures of you in your car seat as daddy put you in the car.

calming
PACI

At first we tried to avoid giving you the pacifier, but how can we deprive you of something that you so greatly love to do? As soon as you get it you relax and sometimes we even hear a little sigh. You enjoy your paci the most in the car.

Look through stacks of photos to see small trends, like the love of a particular pacifier.

relaxing
BATH

Everything we read says that babies only need a bath once or twice a week but you love them so much that we usually give you one everyday. As part of our bedtime routine, your big brother helps with your bath. You just sit back and relax.

peaceful
SLEEP

Yes, your life is sweet! You sleep often during the day. Some favorite spots to snooze are in mommy or daddy's arms, your swing, and your bassinet. I was happy and surprised at how well you slept at night even at such a young age.

Keep your accents simple. Erin printed images from a dingbat font and mounted them on cardstock.

first-year album

Lisa Storms found a great way to tackle the growing pile of photos of her son Owen's first year. She put them all in a Scrapworks Bay Box album. The album system features a hybrid of photo sleeves and scrapbook page protectors in lots of layout options, from a full 12 × 12" page to one page with several 4 × 6" pockets.

1. Gather and group your photos. You can group them by theme, by date or time, or even by orientation—some page protectors require all vertical or all horizontal images.

2. Decide where you'll put your title and journaling on each page, then print them out or write on a block that will fit in the designated pocket.

3. Start loading your album. Add accents if you like, but be careful—the added thickness can make it difficult to slide your photos in and out of the smaller pockets.

SOURCES Album: Scrapworks. Patterned paper: KI Memories ("Big Sister" stripes; second, fourth, fifth, sixth, seventh blocks of stripes on title page; dots, calendars/clocks), Making Memories (pink and green "lullaby" stripes), Sandylion (blue and green stripes), Scrapworks ("everyday life" stripes). Fonts: Wingdings (clocks), Go Long ("5 months old"), Brandywine ("going," "gone," lullaby lyrics), Pegsanna ("Lullaby") off the Internet, Century Gothic (journaling, "sister," Arial ("Big Heart,") Times New Roman "Big"), Book Antiqua ("Big Heart" journaling). Stickers: BasicGrey ("everyday life") Chatterbox ("a typical day"), Autumn Leaves (epoxy circle). Rubber stamps: Magenta (sheet music), Hero Arts (word heart). Tag: We R Memory Keepers. Charm: Making Memories. Punch: EK Success. Design: Lisa Storms.

Make a title page to fit in one of the system's full 12 × 12" protectors.

Use a page pulled from a daily planner to detail your baby's schedule.

Rather than resizing photos, spice up larger pockets with patterned paper.

Print a title and trim it to fit one of your pockets. Lisa added journaling in strips for a bit of character.

Personality

& relationships

PRESERVE THAT POUT,
and save that smile.
Chronicle your little one's
developing persona as well as
his role within your family. Look
to the scrapbook pages in this
chapter for creative ways to
capture your baby's sunny
disposition, endearing quirks,
and, yes, mood swings.

Keep the ink in pens flowing freely by storing them horizontally and always with their lids on.

Happy by Kelly Noel

Kelly's handwritten journaling on bright cardstock strips adds emphasis and interest to her words.

TIP: Look no further than your patterned-paper stash for snazzy shapes—like the flowers Kelly used—you can cut out and add to your layout for extra punch.

SOURCES Cardstock: Bazzill Basics Paper. Patterned paper: Me and My Big Ideas. Stickers, brads: Making Memories. Pen: Sanford. Ribbon: Offray.

HAPPY

You have been through so much already in your short little life — cat scans, therapy, reflux, milk allergy — yet you still remain one of the happiest babies we've ever seen!

Great Mother by Ashley Gailey

Every parent can relate to Ashley's musings about her adjustments to the routine of caring for a newborn.

TIP: Reinforce a design theme by selecting similarly shaped items, as Ashley did with her circular accents and funky circle-print paper.

SOURCES Cardstock: Bazzill Basics Paper. Patterned paper: Autumn Leaves. Font: Children (dingbat) off the Internet, Century Gothic (text). Conchos, stud: Scrapworks.

Great mother or total sucker?

Heck. I don't know...

I just can't stand to hear her scream, which she does a lot.
A LOT. Yup, she loves to be held.
It sure makes getting things done difficult.
On the upside I'm going to have super buff arms soon.
I don't know what I would do without the Baby Bjorn.
Some days I have to tote her around in it for hours.
I know she'll grow out of this phase soon enough.
Right? RIGHT? July 2005 – Ava, five weeks old

B Yourself by Nia Reddy

A greeting card inspired Nia to create a page that would remind her son to be himself.

TIP: Make a black-and-white photo stand out by accenting your page with bright colors.

SOURCES Patterned paper: Scenic Route Paper Co. (green dot), Anna Griffin (black dot, gingham). Fonts: Flip Flop (title), Zurich (journaling) off the Internet. Rub-on: Daisy D's Paper Co. Metal-rim tags: Making Memories.

Aiden, as your mama there are times when I sit back and wonder where this life of yours is going to take you (that is when I am not cleaning crayon off the walls or running for dear life trying to catch up with you)

You seem to have gotten a good start in life - You are surrounded by a loving family, you live in a city that fosters new experiences every single day, and you have that creative spirit that is destined to take you magical places.

I want you to remember that wherever you chose to go in life, you must always do it for yourself. Speak, walk, live, see, be and think for yourself. Create your own destiny and follow the path that you choose. Remember little man, this is on the beginning — the rest of your life is up to you. Live it well.

A Father's Love

A daddy's girl and you can't even crawl yet. It's so wonderful to watch your relationship develop. You've got Daddy wrapped around your tiny little finger; you both look upon each other with such adoration. You give him big smiles and coos when he sees you in the morning or when he comes home from work. You love your special times with him, you trust him completely, and the bond is evident even to complete strangers.

A Father's Love by Courtney Kelly

Thin strips of ribbon and several patterned papers frame a beautiful photo of Courtney's husband holding their baby daughter.

TIP: Cut one side of paper-strip borders with decorative-edge scissors to give a simple page zip.

SOURCES Patterned paper, ribbon: American Crafts. Fonts: Verdigris by Autumn Leaves (title), Century Gothic (journaling). Chipboard accent: Heidi Swapp.

Place text perfectly by printing it on plain paper and holding it over your planned page on a light box or against a window.

Thankful for You by Leslie Lightfoot

Leslie whipped up a quick striped background for this page about her daughter's sweet temperament by stitching strips of patterned paper to a sheet of plain cardstock.

TIP: Apply digital borders to photos or brush a bit of acrylic paint on prints for an artsy, aged effect.

SOURCES Patterned paper: Autumn Leaves (green), K&Company (maroon). Transparency, epoxy accent: Creative Imaginations. Font: Aunt Marie ("thank you") by Autumn Leaves, Times New Roman (journaling). Label holders: Creative Imaginations (large), Making Memories (small). Acrylic accents: Doodlebug Design. Acrylic paint, brads: Making Memories.

My Little Miss by Nasilele Holland

Nasilele selected large photos of her friend Keoni to show off the "daughter I never had."

TIP: Add a title to your photo using photo-editing software, stickers, or rub-ons.

SOURCES Cardstock: Bazzill Basics Paper. Patterned paper: Rusty Pickle. Fonts: Zaphino (script), Bodoni XT (title, journaling) off the Internet. Ribbon: May Arts. Punch: EK Success.

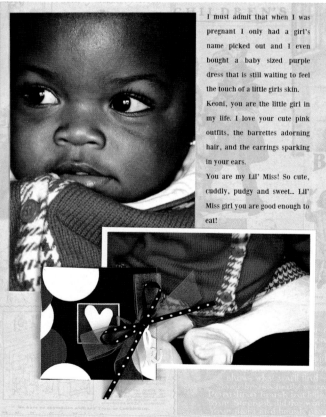

I must admit that when I was pregnant I only had a girl's name picked out and I even bought a baby sized purple dress that is still waiting to feel the touch of a little girls skin.

Keoni, you are the little girl in my life. I love your cute pink outfits, the barrettes adorning hair, and the earrings sparking in your ears.

You are my Lil' Miss! So cute, cuddly, pudgy and sweet... Lil' Miss girl you are good enough to eat!

little stinker
crazy

bugaboo
sweet boy
tarson woyd

Big boy mister

POOPY
carson boy
baby

mr. chubs
BUBBA
Noisy boy

1 month
3 months
8 months
11 months

Babies are sensitive to light, so use natural light or bounce your camera's flash off a ceiling or wall when photographing your little one.

C by Rebecca Cooper

Rebecca varied the color, case, and size of the font she used to type up this fun list of nicknames her family has for her son, Carson.

TIP: Create custom text effects using your word-processing program. Print a draft on plain paper first to make sure your spacing is right, then print directly onto your background paper.

$ SOURCES Patterned paper, metal letter, ribbon: American Crafts. Fonts: Zurich ("bugaboo," "poopy," "Carson boy," "bubba") off the Internet, Avant Garde (all other).

What Do You See? by Sheila Doherty

Sheila snapped several shots of her son looking out the window to create a page about his curiosity with the world around him.

TIP: Create a ghosted-back title like Sheila's in your word-processing software, or fake the look with watercolor pencils and a blender pen.

SOURCES Patterned paper: KI Memories (green floral, polka dot, solid green), Chatterbox (stripe, orange floral). Font: Gill Sans. Stickers: Mrs. Grossman's. Acrylic paint: Delta (Ceramcoat). Tag: EK Success. Brads, rub-on letters: Making Memories. Ribbon: Michaels.

> Search the *Web* for *free* digital goodies. I found a program called The Font Thing that helps me choose *fonts* in a *flash.*
>
> Erin Roe, 2006 Creative Team member

Your Genes by Jen Lessinger

Jen designed this page to show off her son's resemblance to his grandfather by using cute photos of the two of them together.

TIP: Introduce an accent color with embellishments, like the line and triangles Jen used here. The splash of light blue draws attention to the triangles as they direct the eye to the photos.

SOURCES Patterned paper: CB2. Transparency: Autumn Leaves. Font: American Typewriter off the Internet. Chipboard accents: Heidi Swapp (triangles, "your," "it's pretty"), Scenic Route Paper Co. ("genes," "clear").

Heaven Sent by Renee Villalobos-Campa

This sweet photo of siblings speaks volumes about their relationship, so Renee enlarged it to fill most of the page.

TIP: Take the guesswork out of coordinating papers. Renee simply cut up one sheet of quilted-squares paper to create her individual pieces.

SOURCES Cardstock: Provo Craft. Patterned paper: Daisy D's Paper Co. Font: 1942 Report off the Internet. Acrylic paint: Delta. Metal letters: Making Memories. Label holder: Creative Imaginations. Brads, buttons, cloth label, photo turn: Junkitz. Trim: Offray.

Caution by Mindy Bush

Two large images, taken just moments apart, set the stage for Mindy's layout about her daughter's mood swings.

TIP: For a complete picture of your child's personality, include all of her moods—not just the good ones.

 SOURCES Patterned paper: Autumn Leaves. Font: Times New Roman.

CAUTION

Possible meltdown at any moment.
My darling daughter, you run on pure emotion. It's as if you can see what your feeling. just by the expressions you make. Within minutes you can go from a smile to tears.

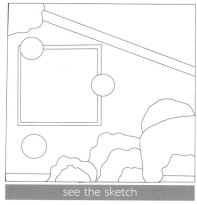

see the sketch

Rockin' Uncle Rhett by Alexis Hardy

Alexis' vibrant layout reflects her brother's energetic spirit, as well as the special bond he shares with her daughter.

TIP: Make the date part of your design. Alexis wrote out the month and drew an arrow pointing to the date on the measuring-tape border along the bottom.

SOURCES Patterned paper: American Crafts (white leaves, maroon), Karen Foster Design (measuring tape). Pen: Signo (white journaling). Color pencils: Crayola.

> Keep your *camera* handy to take pictures of the new things your baby does. I've missed many photo *opportunities* because my baby *quickly* moved on to something *new* before I caught him on film.
>
> Lisa Storms, 2006 Creative Team member

COO FOR THE CAMERA

Capturing your baby's personality on film isn't always easy. Try these simple tips from photographer moms to help you get picture-perfect results.

• **Diffuse the situation.** Soft lighting complements little ones' delicate features. Babies are sensitive to bright lights, so use natural light or bounce your flash off a ceiling, a wall, or a piece of white foam-core board to get a softer effect.

• **Flex your trigger finger.** Take lots of photos; don't wait for a "perfect" look or mood. Babies grow so quickly, and you can never have enough photos of that first year.

• **Go for spontaneity.** It's a rare baby that wants to pose for the camera, so go for unstaged shots. Yawning, giggling, and even pouting make for better images than stiff stances.

• **Make it a family effort.** Show relationships by including siblings, grandparents, and other relatives in shots. Watch how they interact and capture a moment when they're focused on one another rather than the camera.

• **Use a prop.** Give Baby a stuffed animal or favorite toy to keep him relaxed and give him something to focus on.

Give new papers an aged look by skimming the edges with brown stamping ink.

Sean from A to Z by Pam Callaghan

The alphabet forms the basis for 26 special words that Pam used to describe her son as he approached his first birthday.

TIP: Create your own letter blocks by stamping letters onto scraps of patterned paper. Cut them into different-size rectangles with decorative-edge scissors.

SOURCES Patterned paper: Autumn Leaves (harlequin, red stripe, red floral), Karen Foster Design (blue stripe), Melissa Frances (vintage print). Rubber stamps: Wendi Speciale. Ink: Ranger Industries. Flowers: Prima Marketing. Ribbon: May Arts (sheer brown, blue), Venus Industries (blue with brown dots). Brads: Making Memories.

Best Big Brother by Stacy Sattler

A large photo of Stacy's children dominates this page about the duo's relationship, but the small details—like the handwritten tag and stitched-together paper scraps—add to the character of the page.

TIP: When creating a page about a sibling relationship, include the older sibling's handwriting to create an immediate connection.

$ SOURCES Patterned paper: BasicGrey (stripe), KI Memories (other). Font: Times New Roman. Die cut: My Mind's Eye. Ink: Clearsnap.

Olivia & G.G. by Melissa Inman

On this layout, Melissa left lots of room to tell the story of her daughter's first encounter with her great-grandmother.

TIP: Highlight specific words and phrases in long blocks of journaling by printing them in a different color.

SOURCES Cardstock: Bazzill Basics Paper. Patterned paper: Me and My Big Ideas (pink), Daisy D's Paper Co. (green floral), The Paper Company (floral). Font: Avenir. Stickers: Chatterbox (letters), EK Success (epoxy). Slide mount: Design Originals. Ribbon: Making Memories.

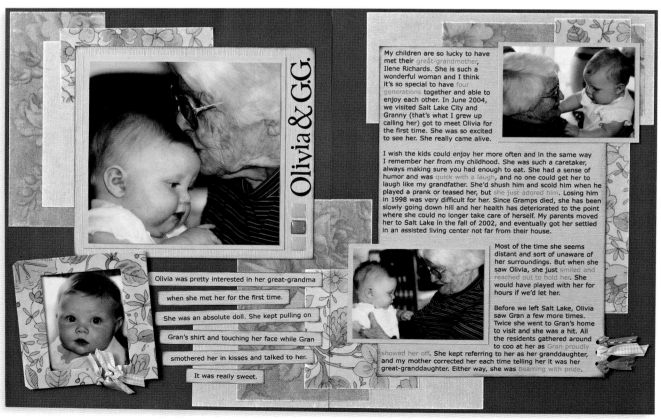

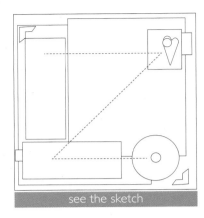

see the sketch

Unbreakable Bond by Greta Hammond

All of Greta's hopes and dreams before her daughter's arrival still couldn't prepare her for how she felt when she took this photo of her son holding his new little sister.

TIP: Place accents—like the top photo corner, heart accent, title, and flower on this page—in strategic positions to help the eye move through the layout in a Z pattern.

SOURCES Patterned paper: Scenic Route Paper Co. (orange), Chatterbox (cream). Font: Californian FB by Microsoft. Die, die-cutting tool: QuicKutz. Stickers: Scrapworks. Rub-ons: Autumn Leaves. Acrylic paint, tag: Making Memories. Chipboard letters: Heidi Swapp. Photo corners, flower: Chatterbox. Buttons: Bazzill Basics Paper (heart), Chatterbox (flower).

Hand off your *camera* often to friends or family to take photos of *you* with the baby.

Lisa Storms, 2006 Creative Team member

One Sweet Friend by Polly Maly

As Polly took photos of her newborn niece, Allison, the family pet came to supervise. Polly captured a shot that hints at the sure-to-blossom friendship between the two.

TIP: Looking for that perfect photo? Use your camera's continous shooting mode to take several shots in rapid succession so you won't miss just the right moment.

SOURCES Cardstock: Bazzill Basics Paper. Patterned paper, die cut: My Mind's Eye. Font: Century Gothic. Stickers: American Crafts (bracket, "friend," "one"). Chipboard accent: Heidi Swapp. Ribbon: SEI. Decorative pin, trim: Making Memories.

Care Giver by Candi Gershon

Candi separated the word "caregiver" into two parts on this digital design about her baby boy's nanny, giving emphasis to both qualities.

TIP: Draw attention to a decorative element by typing or writing your journaling to follow a curve, as Candi did with the flower stem on this page.

SOURCES Software: Adobe Photoshop Elements. Fonts: Afternoon Delight ("care") by Autumn Leaves, Barbara Hand (journaling) off the Internet. Digital elements: Digital Design Essentials (kraft paper, stamped flower, stitching), Design Digitals (yellow paper, chipboard letters), Two Peas in a Bucket (plaque).

She Changed Me by Nicole Gartland

Inspired by her relationship with her second child, Nicole created this page to document how she also is changing in unforeseen ways.

TIP: Apply a couple of coats of dimensional glaze to give depth to a paper title, as Nicole did. Let each coat dry before applying another.

SOURCES Patterned paper: Blue Cardigan. Font: BD Quattra off the Internet. Rubber stamps: Leave Memories. Paint, dimensional glaze: Plaid. Brads, buttons: Making Memories. Page tab: Autumn Leaves.

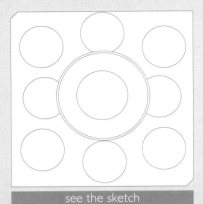

see the sketch

Relationships by Danielle Thompson

Danielle packed in nine photos and oodles of handwritten journaling on this fun and funky layout featuring pics of family members surrounding a central image of her son.

TIP: If writing directly on a layout in pen makes you cringe, first write very lightly with a pencil, then trace over your text with a pen and erase the pencil marks. Just remember to test your paper in advance to make sure the color won't smear when you erase.

SOURCES Patterned paper: Autumn Leaves. Stickers: BasicGrey ("L"), K&Company ("Re"), 7Gypsies ("ation"). Pens: Zig Writer (blue) by EK Success, Sharpie (black) by Sanford. Decorative tape: 7Gypsies.

Mad   by Lisa Dickinson

A bold title treatment and tightly cropped photos of Baby's sour expression clearly convey the theme of Lisa's page.

TIP: Punctuate phrases in list-style journaling by attaching eyelets or brads between your sentences.

$ SOURCES Cardstock: Bazzill Basics Paper. Patterned paper: SEI. Font: Rockwell. Stickers: Mrs. Grossman's. Rub-ons: Li'l Davis Designs. Chipboard letters: Making Memories. Eyelets: The Happy Hammer. Ribbon: Offray.

4 Older Sisters   by Allison Kimball

Allison housed several photos of her son in costume on this page about his role as his sisters' dress-up doll.

TIP: Look for patterns in your photos—such as a facial expression or a special pose with a relative—and group like shots that tell a story about your child's developing personality or relationships.

SOURCES Patterned paper: KI Memories (numbers), Autumn Leaves (floral). Die cuts: KI Memories. Chipboard letters: Making Memories (white), Heidi Swapp (blue). Rubber stamps: PSX (letters), Fontwerks (circle). Flowers: Prima Marketing (solid), Savvy Stamps (blue edge). Printed ribbon, safety pins, photo corner, pearls: Making Memories.

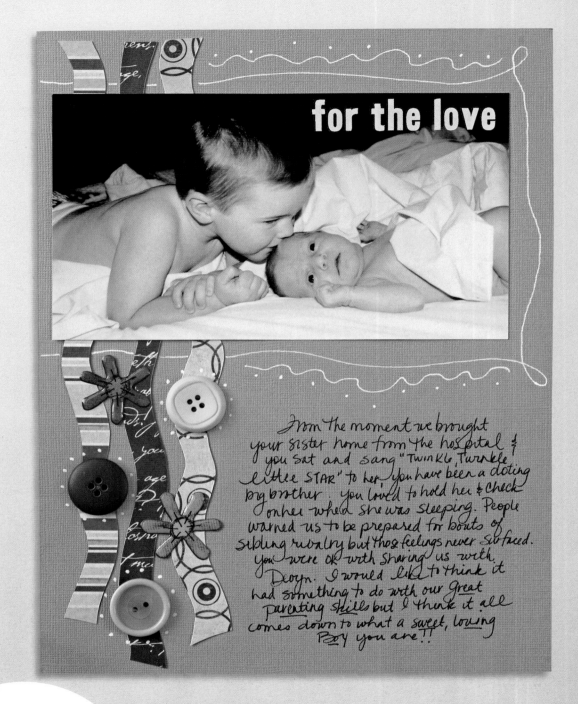

for the love

From the moment we brought your sister home from the hospital & you sat and sang "Twinkle, Twinkle Little Star" to her, you have been a doting big brother. You loved to hold her & check on her when she was sleeping. People warned us to be prepared for bouts of sibling rivalry but those feelings never surfaced. You were ok with sharing us with Devyn. I would like to think it had something to do with our great parenting skills but I think it all comes down to what a sweet, loving boy you are!!

Sharpen an often-used paper punch by punching through a piece of aluminum foil a few times. Help out a sticky punch by punching through wax paper.

For the Love by Vicki Boutin

To give this page about her son's new big-brother status freeform style, Vicki cut wavy strips of paper and decorated with hand-drawn doodles and mismatched buttons.

TIP: Simple squiggly lines and dots are wonderful ways to highlight photos or other elements and bring more of your personality—or your subject's—into your layouts.

SOURCES Cardstock: Bazzill Basics Paper. Patterned paper: Scenic Route Paper Co. Stickers: All My Memories. Buttons: Autumn Leaves.

minor adjustments

My sweet Madi…it's plain to see that you are having some trouble adjusting to life with a little brother. At first I was worried that you would take things out on him, but instead you've decided to unleash your anger on Dad and I. For 3 years and 14 days you were undoubtedly the centre of attention and the only baby in the family. Now that Luke is here, there are people oohing and aaaahing at him like they did with you. Since he came home, I've noticed a real change in your personality. You don't like to listen and you have started talking back much of the time for no real reason. I know that this is simply your way of telling us that you miss all the attention and that's okay. I know it's a phase you're in that hopefully won't last too long. I'm just happy that you are so loving and gentle with your little brother and you haven't even said a bad word about him yet. I'm sorry that you feel left out and somewhat neglected right now. It'll get better in time, I promise. You'll always be my favourite little girl.

CHEER UP

Minor Adjustments by Melissa Chapman

Her daughter's reaction to sharing the spotlight inspired Melissa to create this relationship page.

TIP: Include semiserious subjects in your scrapbooks, but have fun with those memories, too, as Melissa did with the dramatic (but cute) photo of her daughter.

 SOURCES Cardstock: Bazzill Basics Paper (orange), Prism Papers (green, white, blue). Font: Futura. Sticker: Making Memories.

Josiah by Sharon Laakkonen

Three same-size photos share the space on Sharon's layout about her son's personality. By alternating black-and-white shots with a color one and backing each with a patterned paper, Sharon keeps the three from dissolving into each other.

TIP: Spice up machine-stitched borders by alternating thread colors. Reluctant to drag out the sewing machine? Outline with colored pens for a similar look.

SOURCES Patterned paper: Imagination Project (floral, stripe), Chatterbox (linen colors). Font: Chatter by Two Peas in a Bucket. Ink: Ranger Industries. Brads: Queen & Co. Flowers: Prima Marketing. Chipboard letters: Heidi Swapp. Cotton tape: Imagination Project.

Write your journaling by hand. You'll save time by not needing to *format* your text on the computer.

Leah Fung, contributing editor

the two
ajesty will onl

your temperament truly amazes me. you are so
relaxed and mellow. i've rarely heard you fuss.
and i don't think i've heard you cry at all.
we are so blessed to have you. not just because
you're quiet and easy to be around. we just love
you because you're you. our greyson thomas.

blessed to
have you.
in our lives

e officers of
strained

calm & cool

Use papers with large, bold patterns as accent papers and those with more subtle patterns for page backgrounds.

Calm & Cool by Becky Novacek

Becky machine-stitched punched circles, ribbon, and a title to create this textural page about her son's mellow personality.

TIP: Tack down embellishments with temporary adhesive, then machine-stitch over them. Just be careful to keep your needle adhesive-free.

SOURCES Patterned paper: Autumn Leaves, Cloud 9 Design, Heidi Grace Designs. Stickers: Heidi Grace Designs. Die cut: Jenni Bowlin Studio. Flower: Fancy Pants Designs. Punch: Fiskars.

Mia by Michelle Guray

Michelle dressed up a special black-and-white photo of her and her daughter by placing floral accents along a curved edge she cut along the left side of the page.

TIP: When embellishing a curved edge, keep the final size in mind so your design will still fit within your page protector. Place a full-size sheet under your design when adding the accents as a reminder of your boundaries.

SOURCES Cardstock: Bazzill Basics Paper. Patterned paper: KI Memories (dots), Autumn Leaves (all other). Font: Modern Type by Autumn Leaves. Die cuts: Autumn Leaves. Rub-ons: 7Gypsies (swirls, dots), American Crafts ("i," "a"). Chipboard accent: Heidi Swapp ("M"). Rubber stamp, ink: Close To My Heart. Acrylic paint: DecoArt. Paper flowers: Doodlebug Design. Photo corner: Canson. Brads: Making Memories.

Sweet Jackson

by Amy Howe

A close-up photo inspired Amy to create this layout about her son's emerging personality.

TIP: Add pizzazz to a white photo border by embellishing the edge with machine stitching. For eye-catching contrast, use colored thread.

SOURCES Page kit: Lasting Impressions. Cardstock: Bazzill Basics Paper. Fonts: Century Gothic. Chipboard letters: BasicGrey. Buttons: Buttons Galore. Punch: Marvy Uchida.

digital album

Let's face it: The thought of putting together an entire baby album can be daunting. But there are plenty of software programs that can simplify the process. Several programs allow you to simply select the photos and templates you want to use, and they do the rest.

As someone who creates many of her scrapbook pages on the computer, Heather Melzer was intrigued with the idea of a program that would allow her to design an entire album digitally without putting a damper on her creativity. Using the Epson Storyteller kit, Heather created three versions of the same album so you can see how ideal the system is—whether you want to add just a little personal flavor or a lot.

The kit comes with everything you need to create a hardback album: software, photo paper, a bound book to house your printed photo pages, and a glossy wraparound cover. The software includes several page templates to choose from and lets you drop up to 200 photos into your book while it positions and sizes each image automatically.

FOR THE FASTEST ALBUM, Heather simply chose a template from the program and loaded her digital photos into it. After selecting the photos, the software arranged the layouts for her. She added titles and journaling in the spaces in a font chosen by the program. Although the program does much of the work for you, you can customize pages, swapping photos in and out of spots to make your favorites the stars. Heather loved that when she moved photos the captions moved as well, but she felt a bit limited since she couldn't change the typestyle or size of her text.

SOURCES Album kit: Epson. Design: Heather Melzer.

Mix and match page templates for a custom look with little effort.

Quickly put together a page of favorite photos using a template with lots of photo spots.

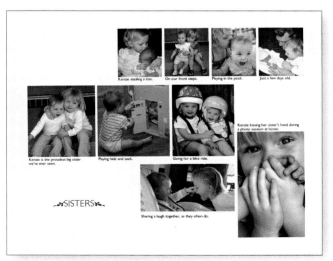

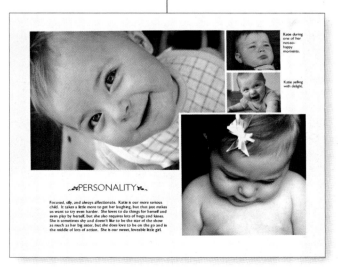

IN HER SECOND VERSION, Heather used the Storyteller program to create the layouts but added embellishments to the pages after she printed them. She created her own titles in a font that was different from the one in the Storyteller template and added rub-ons to dress up the pages and cover.

SOURCES Album kit: Epson. Font: Caecilia Roman off the Internet. Rub-ons: Autumn Leaves. Design: Heather Melzer.

katie's birth day

Katie was born on November 4, 2004 at 10:10am. She weighed 7lbs, 13 ounces and was 20 inches long. Mom was in labor for 12 hours and delivered for about 3. She was placed on Mom's belly as soon as she was born and Dad was right there, too. Grandma and Grandpa Wilson brought Kenzie to see her new baby sister very shortly after she was born and Grandma and Grandpa Melzer and Aunt Lori arrived just a few hours later. Everyone was so excited to finally meet her.

family

We are so lucky to live so close to our families. Both sets of parents, and often our siblings, come out to visit the girls at least once a week. They can't stand to be away from Katie too long because she's always up to something new. She loves playing with her cousins, and her aunts and uncles love to make her laugh. She has two sets of very loving grandparents that just can't get enough of her.

Stick to rub-ons and stickers. Bulky accents won't work well in these booklike albums.

Change the title styles by covering the originals with ones printed in a different font.

sisters

personality

Focused, silly, and always affectionate. Katie is our more serious child. It takes a little more to get her laughing, but that just makes us want to try even harder. She loves to do things for herself and even play by herself, but she also requires lots of hugs and kisses. She is sometimes shy and doesn't like to be the star of the show as much as her big sister, but she does love to be on the go and in the middle of lots of action. She is our sweet, loveable little girl.

FOR HER THIRD VARIATION, Heather used the kit materials—photo paper, hard-bound book, wraparound cover—but not the software, opting to use her preferred photo-editing software instead. The result is an album that's more reflective of her style, although it definitely took more time to create.

SOURCES Album kit: Epson. Software: Digital Image Pro. Fonts: Misproject (titles) off the Internet, Century Gothic (journaling). Digital elements: Two Peas In a Bucket (swirl brushes, papers), Heather Ann Designs (white cardstock, scalloped edge). Design: Heather Melzer.

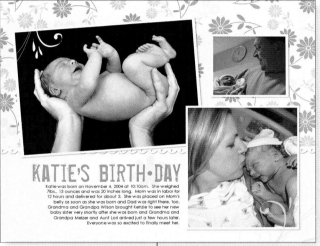

KATIE'S BIRTH·DAY

Katie was born on November 4, 2004 at 10:10am. She weighed 7lbs., 13 ounces long. Mom was in labor for 12 hours and delivered for about 3. She was placed on Mom's belly as soon as she was born and Dad was right there, too. Grandma and Grandpa Wilson brought Kenzie to see her new baby sister very shortly after she was born and Grandma and Grandpa Melzer and Aunt Lori arrived just a few hours later. Everyone was so excited to finally meet her.

FAMILY

We are so lucky to live so close to our families. Both sets of parents, and often our siblings, come out to visit the girls at least once a week. They can't stand to be away from Katie too long because she's always up to something new. She loves playing with her cousins, and her aunts and uncles love to make her laugh. She has two sets of very loving grandparents that just can't get enough of her.

> Add color to digital layouts with "patterned-paper" backgrounds and decorative brushes.

> Vary the structure of the template page designs by resizing and tilting some photos.

SISTERS

We honestly weren't sure how Mackenzie would take to having a new baby sister in the house, but she turned out to be the proudest big sister we've ever seen. She loves to give Katie hugs and she does everything she can to make her laugh (which makes her laugh, too). Katie is a little overwhelmed by her very energetic older sister, but she loves to follow her all around the house to see what she's up to. They're so lucky to have each other and we hope they become great friends.

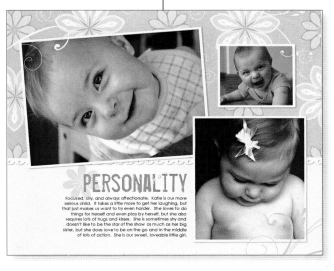

PERSONALITY

Focused, silly, and always affectionate. Katie is our more serious child. It takes a little more to get her laughing, but that just makes us want to try even harder. She loves to do things for herself and even play by herself, but she also requires lots of hugs and kisses. She is sometimes shy and doesn't like to be the star of the show as much as her big sister, but she does love to be on the go and in the middle of lots of action. She is our sweet, loveable little girl.

Special events

WHETHER IT'S his first birthday or first Halloween, don't forget to record all of Baby's big days. Keep the joy of special events alive by scrapbooking photos of religious ceremonies, holidays, and birthdays.

Add weight to your handwriting by tracing over your letters a second time. Don't worry about making it perfect—gaps make the letters bolder.

Ava's First Chanukah   by Jen Lessinger

Jen made the photos the focus on this page about a special Chanukah for her friends' daughter. The brightly colored images stand out against the white background, and the patterned-paper accents provide character without overwhelming the images.

TIP: Use adhesive foam to make an element—like the Star of David Jen made from two triangles of patterned paper—pop off your page.

$ **SOURCES** Cardstock: Bazzill Basics Paper. Patterned paper: Me and My Big Ideas (stripe), SEI (vellum circles). Font: American Typewriter off the Internet. Stickers: American Crafts. Chipboard accents: Heidi Swapp. Woven flourish: Autumn Leaves.

Five months is a bit too young to light the menorah ... but not too young to eat wrapping paper!

A BABY MAKES EVERYTHING EXCEPTIONAL.

AVA'S first ✡

chanukah

1st Birthday Fun

On Katie's 1st Birthday, we had both of our families over for a night of fun. We ate, played games and had homemade cake. Uncle Mike came in for a surprise visit from school and revealed himself by jumping out of a box in the garage. The cousins had a great time playing Elefun and Kenzie ate way too many chips and dip (as usual). A wonderful time was had by all, especially Katie :)

1st Birthday Fun by Heather Melzer

A magazine layout inspired Heather to showcase multiple scenes from her daughter's birthday party on one page.

TIP: If you're having trouble ruling out photos, go with multiple small images. Just be sure each image tells a different part of the story.

SOURCES Software: Microsoft Digital Image Pro. Fonts: Minion (journaling) off the Internet, Ditzy (title) by Two Peas in a Bucket. Digital elements: Designer Digitals.

Maeve's Baptism Day by Joy Uzarraga

To capture the memories of a special baptism, Joy chose photos that set the scene, showed the action, and zoomed in on the guest of honor.

TIP: To match your font color to your patterned paper in image-editing software, scan the paper and use the eyedropper tool to sample a color in the paper. Then apply the color to the text.

SOURCES Cardstock: Bazzill Basics Paper. Patterned paper: American Crafts. Font: Cezanne (title), Garamond (journaling) off the Internet.

Maeve's Baptism Day

11.26.05

Maeve Cavida McGinn, the daughter of Dan & Gina McGinn, was baptized into the Catholic church on a Saturday afternoon at St. Thomas the Apostle Church in Chicago. A reception following the ceremony was held at her Grandpa & Grandma McGinn's house.

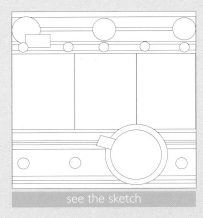

see the sketch

Tiny Tots Santa Claus by Sharon Laakkonen

Sharon captured these close-ups of her son's mixed emotions about wearing his Santa hat during his first Christmas.

TIP: Play with journaling in shapes, but make sure it isn't hard to read. Sharon attached her spiral-shape text with a brad and included a pull tab for easy spinning.

SOURCES Cardstock: Bazzill Basics Paper. Patterned paper: Scenic Route Paper Co. Ink: Clearsnap. Plastic accents: Heidi Swapp. Buttons: Autumn Leaves. Woven tabs: Scrapworks.

Shortcut by Amy Licht

Amy's bright palette is perfect for a fun page about her daughter Abby's delicious discovery of frosting.

TIP: Minimize the distractions of busy paper by using it as a background and grouping other elements on a solid color so they're easier to see.

SOURCES Cardstock: Bazzill Basics Paper. Patterned paper: 7Gypsies. Fabric paper: Michael Miller Memories. Font: CAC One-Seventy (journaling), Hootie (subtitle) off the Internet. Chipboard letters, wood flower: Li'l Davis Designs. Ribbon: May Arts. Brad: Happy Hammer.

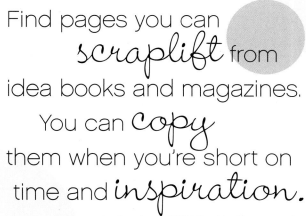

Find pages you can *scraplift* from idea books and magazines. You can *copy* them when you're short on time and *inspiration.*

Jen Lessinger, 2006 Creative Team member

Thanks by Sarah Klemish

All dolled up for Thanksgiving, Sarah's adorable niece is the center of this streamlined design that's quick to assemble but conveys a powerful message.

TIP: Make a big statement on a plain background with a few strips of stylish patterned paper. It's a great way to use up scraps.

SOURCES Patterned paper: Chatterbox. Font: Bell Gothic off the Internet. Chipboard letters: Heidi Swapp.

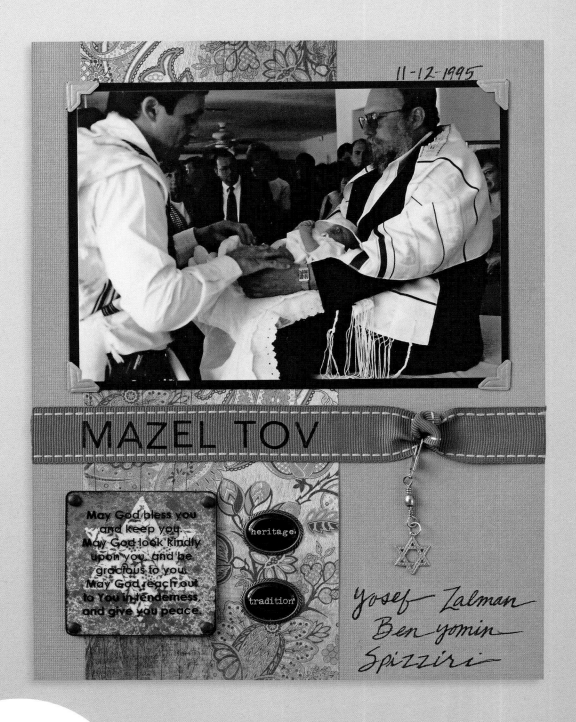

11-12-1995

MAZEL TOV

May God bless you and keep you. May God look kindly upon you, and be gracious to you. May God reach out to You in tenderness, and give you peace.

heritage

tradition

Yosef Zalman Ben yomin Spizziri

Mazel Tov by Allison Landy

Allison set a solemn tone with subdued papers for this page about the bris of a friend's son.

TIP: Jazz up your ribbon by adding rub-ons, which will stick well to many materials.

SOURCES Cardstock: Die Cuts with a View. Patterned paper: BasicGrey. Rub-ons: Making Memories. Rubber stamp: Stampin' Up!. Ink, embossing powder: Tsukineko. Dye: Ranger Industries. Epoxy accents, frames: Li'l Davis Designs. Chipboard accent: Technique Tuesday. Photo corners: Canson. Ribbon: May Arts. Brads: The Happy Hammer.

Worried about damaging a one-of-a-kind print? Make a duplicate or attach it to the page with photo corners.

You wore a Hershey's Kiss costume for your first Halloween. I had borrowed it from a friend whose daughter had worn it two years prior. It fit you perfectly and the turtleneck and tights you wore underneath were the icing on the cake. You were adorable. I was able to take a few pictures in the afternoon before it got too dark. As the evening came upon us, Daddy and I took you around the cul-de-sac with your brother. You had no interest in the hat part of your costume, so you promptly pulled it off. Without it you looked more like a space egg than a kiss, but you were still cute as can be.

Absolutely delicious.

First Halloween Kiss by Candi Gershon

Babies in cute costumes always make sweet subjects for Halloween scrapbook pages, and these shots of Candi's dressed-up daughter prove the point.

TIP: Group your main elements on a solid background so they stand out, and then mat the cardstock with patterned paper for a framed effect.

SOURCES Software: Photoshop Elements 3. Digital elements: Digital Design Essentials (paper, chipboard letters, ribbon). Shabby Princess (staple, tab). Fonts: Sandra ("Halloween") by Autumn Leaves, Myriad Pro (journaling) off the Internet.

A Smile So Big by Mindy Bush

With a photo this memorable, Mindy wanted to enlarge it to properly show off that great grin.

TIP: Be picky about which photos you enlarge. Don't push a print copy too far, and make sure the resolution on digital files is high enough to support a bigger size.

SOURCES Patterned paper: Wild Asparagus (floral), K&Company (polka dot), 7Gypsies (script), BasicGrey (red). Fonts: SBC Stone Inscription (title) off the Internet, Arial (journaling).

A SMILE SO BIG HER EYES DISAPPEAR!

Christmas 2004

We took this photo of Alora on Christmas Day. It is a perfect shot that shows one of my favorite things about her... her trademark Bradshaw smile! A smile so big that her eyes disappear! Her smile is definitely contagious!

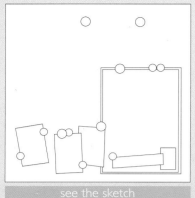

see the sketch

Christening Gown by Jennifer Bourgeault

Delicate details and a neutral palette create just the right backdrop for a page about Jennifer's search for the perfect christening outfit.

TIP: Remember your subject. Dark papers and accents would be out of place on a page about such a happy yet solemn event and might overshadow the message.

SOURCES Patterned paper: BasicGrey. Rub-ons: Daisy D's Paper Co. Die cut: K&Company. Beads: Darice. Flowers: Doodlebug Design. Staples: Making Memories. Photo anchor: Junkitz. Brads: SEI (rhinestone), K&Company (pearl).

Cute by Jen Lessinger

A family debate over her son's bunny ears is the focus of this page by Jen, who chose bright orange (to complement the blue in the photo) over a traditional pastel color scheme.

TIP: Create a less-busy background for a title by brushing on a swath of acrylic paint.

SOURCES Cardstock: Die Cuts with a View. Patterned paper: Scrapbook Wizard. Font: Euroference off the Internet. Stickers: Scrapworks. Rub-ons: Autumn Leaves. Acrylic accent: KI Memories. Chipboard letters: Heidi Swapp. Brads: American Crafts. Acrylic paint: Making Memories.

First Thanksgiving by Erin Roe

Erin deviated from the traditional Thanksgiving theme by journaling about all the attention her baby son received on his first visit to meet some of his relatives.

TIP: Though it can be easy to focus on just the baby, don't forget to get pics of of him with others while celebrating his first holidays.

SOURCES Patterned paper: Scenic Route Paper Co. (circles), BasicGrey (orange, blue), Daisy D's Paper Co. (rust). Font: Red Dog by Two Peas in a Bucket. Stickers: Chatterbox. Chipboard letters: We R Memory Keepers. Pens: Sakura of America. Photo Corner: Heidi Swapp.

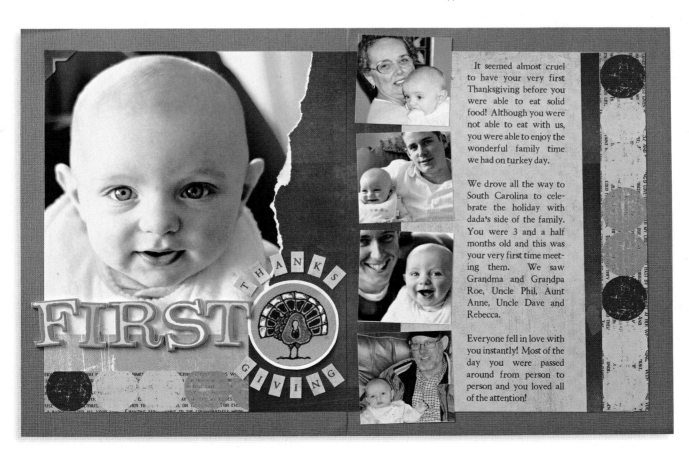

beginning

This was my first Christmas. It's amazing how few presents there are under the tree. My parents were so young then and lived basically hand to mouth. My father was still in college, clamming early mornings to earn a little extra and my mother worked second shift as a nurse at the hospital. Times were tough living on Little East Neck Road in West Islip. They raised us to appreciate the value of a dollar and to not take things for granted. Later on the tree was surrounded by piles of presents, but my parents never forgot how hard it was.

Leave a bit of empty space on your page to give your viewer's eye a place to rest.

Beginning by Celeste Smith

A photo of her own first Christmas inspired Celeste's reflections about her parents' struggle to make ends meet when they were young.

TIP: Work with what you have. Older photos may not enlarge well; a structured design and good use of white space help this photo stand out even though it's small.

SOURCES Cardstock: Bazzill Basics Paper. Patterned paper, flower: Chatterbox. Font: PetraScriptEF (title) off the Internet, Squish (journaling) by Two Peas in a Bucket.

Holly Jolly Christmas by Carrie Cook

A traditional holiday red-and-green color scheme gets a modern update with an infusion of light blue in this digital design about Baby's first Christmas.

TIP: To really capture the glow of holiday lights, turn off your flash and use a slow shutter speed. Just be sure to put your camera on a tripod or steady surface to keep the photo from blurring when you hit the button.

$ **SOURCES** Software: Adobe Photoshop Elements. Digital elements: Shabby Princess.

If you're not sleeping during Baby's *naptime*, scrapbook and *reflect* on the joys of parenthood.

Rhonda Bonifay, 2006 Creative Team member

Father's Day by Nia Reddy

Nia neutralized a distracting background by converting her photo to black-and-white for this layout about her family's first Father's Day with baby Aiden.

TIP: For a quick and easy color scheme, combine two colors that are directly opposite each other on the color wheel, such as green and red, and accent them with black and white.

SOURCES Patterned paper: BasicGrey (large dots), Autumn Leaves (small dots, circles). Vellum: Autumn Leaves. Fonts: Flip Flop (title), Gill Sans Light (journaling) off the Internet. Stickers: American Crafts ("1"), Die Cuts with a View (dots). Brads: Making Memories (small), BasicGrey ("love"). Woven tab: Scrapworks.

It's okay not to use every photo you take. Pick your favorites and share the wealth by giving leftovers to family and friends.

Happy Birthday Baby
by Kelly Noel

Kelly snapped photos of each little guest at her baby's first birthday party and featured them on the page.

TIP: Closely crop photos to remove crazy backgrounds and give wildly different shots a uniform look.

$ **SOURCES** Cardstock: Bazzill Basics Paper. Patterned paper: Provo Craft. Stickers: American Crafts (title), Provo Craft (accents). Pen: Sharpie.

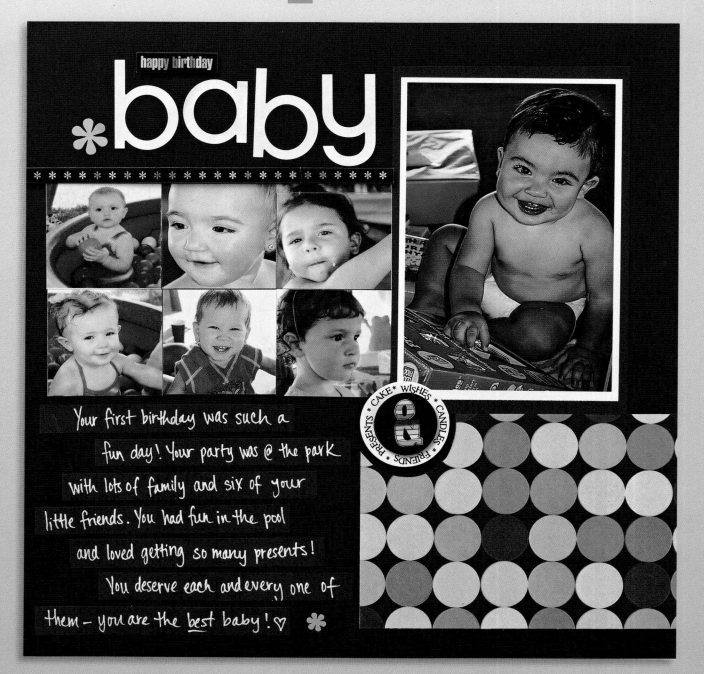

happy birthday

baby

Your first birthday was such a fun day! Your party was @ the park with lots of family and six of your little friends. You had fun in the pool and loved getting so many presents! You deserve each and every one of them — you are the best baby! ♡

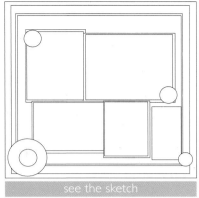

see the sketch

Happy Birthday 2 You!
by JoAnne Bacon

JoAnne used photos of her twins' first birthday to journal about how much she enjoyed seeing them learn and grow together in the first year.

TIP: Hand-cut your title by printing it in reverse text on the back of your paper, then use a craft knife to trim around the outside of the printing before flipping it over and placing it on your page.

SOURCES Cardstock: Bazzill Basics Paper. Patterned paper: Chatterbox. Fonts: Heber (title) by Chatterbox, Journaling Hand (journaling) off the Internet. Chipboard letters, acrylic paint, brads: Making Memories. Flowers: Prima Marketing.

BIRTHDAY PHOTOS

Getting the perfect shot during the excitement of a birthday party can be a tall order. But with a little planning and these helpful hints, you can get the photo you want.

- **Shoot from different angles.** When photographing your baby at his party, try to get on his level so you're eye-to-eye with the action as he tears into the cake. Shoot from above to get the entire cake or to capture happy faces surrounded by discarded wrapping paper without interference from other background elements.

- **Set the scene.** Take a few moments to capture details that make the day special. Snap photos of the cake (before it's devoured), the wrapped presents, and other party attendees. Remember to mix detail shots with overall scene setters, and consider an impromptu group shot or a shot of each guest with the baby. Before the big event, take photos of the party preparations—making the cake, wrapping presents, picking out the little one's outfit. These images enrich your story.

- **Take the shot you want and two more.** Expressions change quickly, and to ensure you get just the smile or squeal you're hoping for, be ready to snap the shutter without notice. Have extra camera batteries and film on hand. If you shoot digitally, make sure your memory card has enough space on it. You don't want to have to download images in the middle of the action.

- **Plan ahead.** If you want a photo of Baby decked out in his birthday duds, take the shot several hours or even the day before the party. It's hard to get a baby to pose for a portrait in the midst of the festivities. Think about placing your child next to a growth chart you can photograph him with next year to show how he's changed.

- **Document relationships.** The natural tendency at first birthday parties is to focus solely on the baby, but photos featuring interaction are an important part of the story.

- **Don't force it.** If your baby won't cooperate for the photo, go ahead and take it anyway—you won't want to miss out on photos capturing the memory just because they aren't perfect.

a year of events

At the end of her baby's first year, Jen Lessinger crafted an album dedicated to the year's special events, from first holidays to the first birthday. To highlight an event from each month of the year, Jen decided on a calendar theme to unify the album.

1. Choose the right album. Because of the theme, Jen knew she didn't need full-size pages—just enough space for a few photos and journaling.

2. Print a calendar for each month onto patterned paper. Use a computer program or an online calendar source to make the task easy.

3. Add photos, journaling, and accents. Circle or highlight with embellishments the dates of when the photos were taken for a quick memory device.

SOURCES Album: Die Cuts with a View. Patterned paper: KI Memories (green), 7Gypsies (black "baptism"), Chatterbox (blue), Autumn Leaves (Christmas), Scenic Route Paper Co. (black "Easter"). Stickers: American Crafts ("t"), Die Cuts with a View (other letters), 7Gypsies (epoxy circle). Rub-ons: Autumn Leaves. Rubber stamps: Magnetic Poetry. Ink: Stewart Superior Corp. Pen: American Crafts. Chipboard accents: Heidi Swapp (stars), Scenic Route Paper Co. (green accents). Design: Jen Lessinger.

Position photos so the date they were taken is visible.

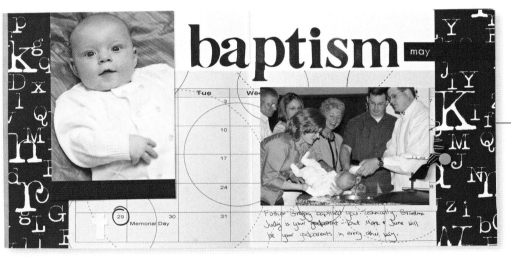

If you don't have a special occasion for every month, just use your favorite photos.

Handwrite captions so you can prepare pages ahead of time and add photos throughout the year.

blessing-day box

To celebrate the blessing day of a friend's baby, Sande Krieger created a unique keepsake—a wood box that houses an accordion album showcasing letters the boy's parents wrote to him. Sande wanted the gift to be something he could display throughout his life to remind him of his parents' love.

1. Decorate the outside of the box with photos, patterned paper, and a title. Inside, fit photos and journaling into the smaller spaces, leaving the larger spot for the accordion album. Seal the surfaces with a coat of decoupage medium.

2. Buy or make an album that will fit in the box's largest section. Sande created more space for her album by including hinged pages that fold out to reveal photos and journaling.

3. Along with letters from Mom, Dad, and other relatives, include photos and the story of the baby's name.

SOURCES Box, mini book, hinges, brads, circle hanger: The Weathered Door. Patterned paper: Scenic Route Paper Co. Stickers: EK Success. Rub-ons, woven label: Making Memories. Stencil: Autumn Leaves. Label maker: Dymo. Design: Sande Krieger.

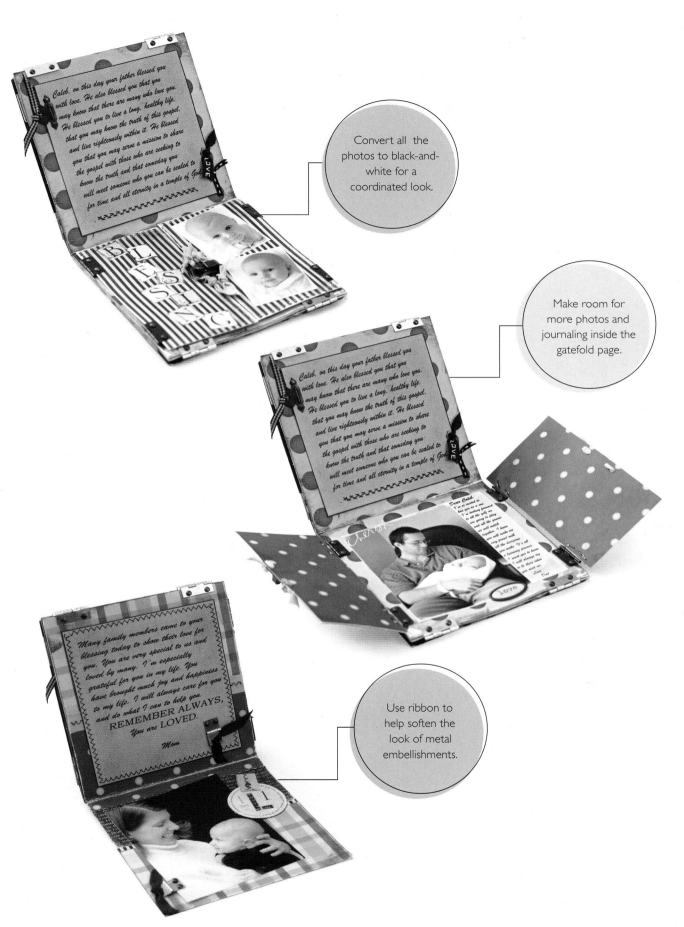

Convert all the photos to black-and-white for a coordinated look.

Make room for more photos and journaling inside the gatefold page.

Use ribbon to help soften the look of metal embellishments.

Gifts for Baby

CONSULT YOUR SCRAPBOOKING supplies and welcome Baby home with a bundle of adorable gifts perfect for wee ones and new moms.

▼ Welcome Baby Basket by Amy Licht

Amy transformed an unfinished wooden basket into a creative corral for baby items using paint and patterned paper.

TIP: After painting the basket, trim paper strips to fit the slats and use decoupage medium to adhere and seal each piece.

SOURCES Patterned paper, stickers, rub-ons: BasicGrey. Acrylic paint: Making Memories. Ribbon: Sopp. Die, die-cutting tool: Sizzix (tag). Corner rounder: EK Success. Adhesive: Zip Dry Glue by Beacon Adhesives.

◄ Circle of Love by Deena Wuest

Deena made this stylish, sentimental bracelet using some of her favorite baby photos, patterned papers, and charms.

TIP: To help her photos stand up to everyday wear and tear, Deena backed her photos with chipboard and covered them with decoupage medium before attaching them to the blank bracelet form.

SOURCES Patterned paper: BasicGrey. Bracelet form: Rings and Things. Charms: K&Company. Jump rings: Making Memories. Acrylic paint and decoupage medium: Plaid.

▲ Alphabet Canvas by Cathy Blackstone

Cathy turned to her scrap stash to create the blocks on this inexpensive custom work of art for her baby's nursery.

TIP: Paint and distress a set of chipboard letters and intersperse them on the canvas, leaving openings for embellishments, photos, artwork, and paper-pieced accents that correspond with the letters.

SOURCES Patterned paper: Autumn Leaves, Imagination Project. Die cuts: 7Gypsies (labels), Autumn Leaves (wings), Scenic Route Paper Co. (arrow), My Mind's Eye (butterfly). Stickers: Autumn Leaves ("3," "9"), BoBunny Press (circle "4"), Doodlebug Design ("6"), K&Company ("8"), KI Memories ("2," "4"), 7Gypsies (frame). Rub-ons: BasicGrey. Chipboard accents: BasicGrey (star), Making Memories (heart), Piggy Tales (alphabet). Stamps: Autumn Leaves (quote stamp), Hero Arts (dotted circle). Brads: Around the Block (dino, flowers), KI Memories (gem), Making Memories (all other). Metal accents: Around the Block (pin, phrase), Making Memories (mouse). Ribbon: KI Memories, May Arts. Sequins: Fibre-Craft Materials Corp. Acrylic coating: Krylon.

▶ Night Light by Polly Maly

Polly purchased a ready-to-decorate night-light kit and customized it by slipping squares of punched vellum into the Plexiglas panel.

TIP: Take advantage of the transparent qualities of vellum by overlapping smaller pieces to create a striped effect.

SOURCES Night-light: Yarn Tree. Punches: EK Success.

Chipboard Baby Mobile
by Leah Fung

For this fun-to-gaze-at mobile, Leah adhered patterned papers to both sides of large chipboard shapes and defined the edges with machine stitching.

TIP: Hang the shapes from one large chipboard shape with rickrack. Be sure to hang the mobile safely out of Baby's reach, and remove it from the crib once your little one can sit up.

SOURCES Patterned paper: Making Memories. Chipboard accents: Making Memories (butterfly, ''a''), Deluxe Designs (all other). Buttons: Chatterbox. Punch: Creative Memories. Ribbon: American Crafts (grosgrain), Michaels (dot). Rickrack: Wrights. Thread: Coats & Clark.

Baby Blocks by Deena Wuest

Deena spelled out her little one's name by priming and painting a set of six unfinished blocks and formatting photos and papers to fit the block faces.

TIP: Digitally format photos and papers to fit on the block faces and add numbers and text to the squares before printing them on photo paper. Or, get a similar look with traditional patterned paper and chipboard letters.

SOURCES Wood blocks: Creative Imaginations. Font: Avante Garde off the Internet. Digital elements: It's a Girl Thing kit by Mindy Terasawa. Software: Adobe Photoshop Elements.

▲ Hanger Labels by Deena Wuest

To brighten up Baby's closet, Deena designed these quick hanger labels with color-coded digital papers and cute animal icons— each hue represents a different clothing size.

TIP: Attach the labels to nursery hangers with adhesive as shown, or bundle them together with ribbon before giving them as a gift.

SOURCES Font: Avante Garde off the Internet. Digital elements: In the Nursery kit (papers) by Katie Pertiet; Jungle Gym Stickers (gorilla), Sweet and Salty Icons (bird, turtle), Little Safari Icons (all other) by Mindy Terasawa. Software: Adobe Photoshop Elements.

◄ Quiet-Time Sign by Amy Licht

To help shush noisy passersby during nap time, Amy created this sign to hang from the doorknob outside her baby's nursery.

TIP: If you can't find the perfect embellishment for your sign, create your own. Amy pieced together basic shapes to make the sailboat on this sign and embellished it with paper trim for the waves.

SOURCES Plaque: Woodline Works Corp. Patterned paper: American Crafts (hearts), Making Memories (check). Font: Century Gothic. Stickers, paper trim: Doodlebug Design. Ribbon: KI Memories (blue dot), Michaels (white). Buttons: Autumn Leaves (green), Target (blue). Floss: DMC Corp. Paint: Krylon.

Baby Block Mobile

by Polly Maly

A sweet addition to a nursery, Polly created this mobile using patterned paper boxes and ribbon hangers.

TIP: Use a box die cut to quickly and easily create boxes with baby-themed patterned papers.

SOURCES Patterned paper: The Paper Patch, K&Company. Hangers: Babies R Us. Die cut: AccuCut.

WANT A
LITTLE MORE?
With the basics behind
you, you're probably raring
to try some of the creative
techniques that can add polish
to any page. Use these easy-to-
follow instructions to create
accents, titles, and more, and
to take your scrapbooking
skills from novice to pro
in no time.

Finishing
touches

YOUR QUALIFIED SUCCESS

You fed yourself pudding with a spoon for the first time tonight for supper. And despite how it appears, you were pretty successful. At 13 months, you don't talk yet but you definitely communicate. Take the pudding, for example. I had a pudding cup for dessert. Once you saw it, you grunted and screamed and threw your food on the floor until you got your own. See? Communication. We started off with each of us using a spoon. We've done that before. But this time, you "got it." You started dipping your spoon and sucking on it. The light bulb went on, and then you wanted to hold the pudding cup and feed yourself. In hindsight, that may not have been the best idea, since the pudding cup eventually ended up on the floor. You definitely enjoyed it though!

Lots of beginning scrapbookers wanting to "print in white" think they need a special type of printer to do so. Not true. For crisp, clean journaling, try white text placed on a dark background. You get a cool effect for pennies and next to no effort.

SOURCES Patterned paper: American Crafts (orange dot), Scrapworks (blue dot). Font: Century Gothic. Chipboard letters: Heidi Swapp. Tags: Avery Dennison. Design: Jen Lessinger.

Print your journaling on matte-finish photo paper for a crisper look than you'll get with cardstock.

1 Open a new Microsoft Word document and create a text box. Change the background color of the text box to orange (or the color you want to use).

2 Type your text inside the box in the default text color (usually black). It's easier to read black on screen so proofread and spell check before changing the color.

3 Highlight the text with your cursor and change the color of the text to white. Print the text box on photo paper, then trim to fit your page.

reverse-print for hand-cutting

Hand-cutting is a cool technique that allows you to create custom titles and other page accents (see page 29). The key to effective hand-cutting is getting a backward print of the text you want to cut out. Follow our directions for using Microsoft Word, or adapt them to fit your word-processing program.

Large, nonfussy fonts work best for hand-cutting.

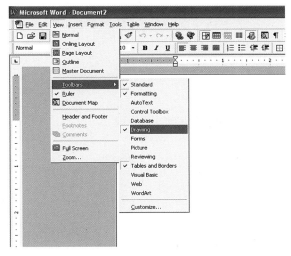

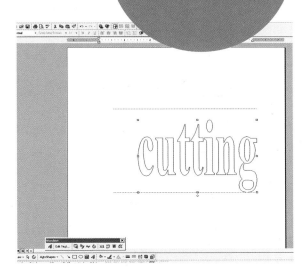

1 Choose the Drawing toolbar from the View menu. Click on the WordArt option (blue slanted letter "A") from the Drawing toolbar.

2 Select the default style of WordArt (outline). Choose your font and type the title. Click OK. Adjust the size of your type by tugging at the corners of the text box.

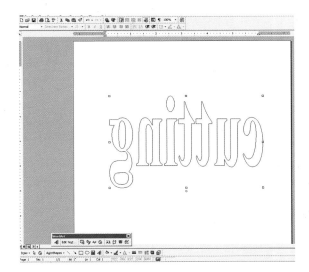

3 Select the Draw option (usually the first item in the Drawing toolbar), click Rotate or Flip, and then pick Flip Horizontal.

4 Make any final size adjustments and print. Print the text on the back of your paper or cardstock so it will be correct once you cut.

Teddy Grahams are one of Katie's favorite snack foods. She especially likes when we buy them in the individual bags because she can help herself to as many as she wants as quickly as she wants. She also loves to share them with her favorite

furry friend (although she knows she isn't supposed to). She won't usually turn any of the flavors away, but choclate is by far her favorite. She loves to run around the house munching on them as she checks things out and plays with her toys. We always keep plenty of them on hand, because Kenzie loves them, too. Oh, and let's not forget about Mom - she's been a fan of them since high school (although she prefers honey). Yum-E!

Sure, it's good for copying photos, but you also can use your scanner to create custom backgrounds and embellishments. Scan sentimental items that are too bulky to add to a layout, such as baby clothes or perhaps an old quilt. It's a great way to preserve the memory of those items as well as keep them intact. Here, Heather Melzer scanned the packaging of her daughter's bear-shape crackers, reinforcing the theme of her story.

SOURCES Font: American Typewriter off the Internet. Ribbon: American Crafts. Chipboard letters: We R Memory Keepers. Design: Heather Melzer.

If you're scanning messy items, place them on top of a piece of glass that can be removed and cleaned (such as the glass from a picture frame).

stamp and heat emboss

If you're stamping a lot, streamline the process by stamping all your images first, then adding the embossing powder, and finally following with the embossing tool.

When heat-embossing an image, give yourself plenty of time for experimentation. You can achieve various effects by changing the color of your ink, the color of your embossing powder, or both. In her sample, Joanna Bolick stamped with blue ink and used a clear embossing powder to preserve the ink color. Had she used blue ink and blue powder, the color would have been more intense.

SOURCES Cardstock: Bazzill Basics Paper. Patterned paper: Me and My Big Ideas. Rubber stamps: FontWerks (flowers), Making Memories (flourish). Ink: Tsukineko. Embossing powder: Stampendous. Pen: Uniball Signo. Design: Joanna Bolick.

What you'll need: a rubber stamp • paper • ink • embossing powder • a shallow tray or pan • a heat tool

1 Ink your stamp with color ink. If your ink pad is smaller than your stamp, press the pad to the stamp rather than the stamp into the tiny pad.

2 Press the stamp to your cardstock, applying even pressure. Avoid rocking the stamp; you may end up with stray ink marks.

3 While the ink is wet, sprinkle clear embossing powder on the image and shake off excess powder into a shallow tray or pan. Pour the excess powder back into the jar.

4 Use a heat tool to melt the powder. If you're creating individual pieces, wait until the embossed area is cool and then cut out the images.

UTEE is an acronym for Ultra Thick Embossing Enamel. You apply it just as you would regular embossing powder, but it's thicker so you can create lumpier embellishments. Joy Uzarraga created a title for her page by pressing an inked word stamp into hot, melted UTEE for a custom look.

SOURCES Cardstock: Bazzill Basics Paper. Rubber stamps: Hero Arts. Ink: Tsukineko (green), Clearsnap (blue). Embossing powder: Ranger Industries. Pen: American Crafts. Photo turns: 7Gypsies. Chipboard shape: Making Memories. Brads: American Crafts. Design: Joy Uzarraga.

Melted UTEE is fun but gets extremely hot. Let the layers cool before you move (or even touch) your creation.

What you'll need: ink (color and embossing) • a rubber stamp • chipboard or cardstock • ultra thick embossing enamel (UTEE) • a shallow tray or pan • a heat tool

1 Trim a piece of chipboard or cardstock to the desired size. Cover the piece with embossing ink.

2 Coat the chipboard with UTEE, working over a shallow tray or pan to catch the excess.

3 Use your heat tool to melt the UTEE. Hold the tool underneath the paper and melt the powder from below to avoid blowing it around. Repeat to build up layers of enamel.

4 Ink your stamp with color ink and press it into the melted UTEE while it's still warm. Leave the stamp in the UTEE until it cools a bit and then remove.

OUR FAMILY LOVES SPENDING SUMMERS OUTDOOR, SO WHEN WE FOUND THE PERFECT CAMPING SPOT IN SUMMER OF 2004, WE ALL KNEW THIS WAS GOING TO BE THE BEST SUMMER EVER. IT'S ONLY ABOUT A FORTY-FIVE MINUTE DRIVE FROM HOME, IT HAS A GREAT SCENIC VIEW, AND LOTS OF ROOM TO PLAY... BUT THE BEST PART IS THE "LAZY RIVER" JUST A SHORT WALK AWAY. THE SHALLOW RIVER PROVIDES LOTS OF FUN ACTIVITIES FOR OUR KIDS TO DO. ON THIS PARTICULAR DAY I CAPTURED BEN TEACHING ETHAN HOW TO SKIP ROCKS. THEY SPENT THE AFTERNOON TRYING TO SKIP ROCKS ACROSS TO THE OTHER SIDE AND BY THE END OF THE DAY ETHAN AND BEN HAD IT DOWN! JUST ANOTHER FAVORITE SUMMER MEMORY

SUMMER
Memories

Inking is a great technique to define the edges of different pattern papers. Lightly rub an ink pad along the edges of cardstock, patterned paper, or even photos to create an aged effect. Christy Tomlinson rubbed gray ink along the edges of each of the patterned papers and the cardstock. Not only does it add a distressed, outdoorsy feel to her layout, but it also helps to unify all of the papers.

SOURCES Cardstock: Bazzill Basics Paper. Patterned paper: Chatterbox. Rub-ons, ribbon: Making Memories. Ink: Clearsnap. Chipboard letters: Li'l Davis Designs. Design: Christy Tomlinson.

Apply the ink with a makeup sponge or ink applicator to get a smoother, dreamier appearance.

first birthday

Alex, when I think of your 1st birthday it is of this moment. When
I opened your door & snapped this picture, the morning of October 8th, 1999.
You were such a happy baby. Smiles. Giggles. Now, year 2 was a different
story! Picture 10/99. Journalling 4/06

Hand-stitching is great when you want a homemade feel or a bit of a whimsical
touch for your page. And you can't go much cheaper than a needle and thread,
so it's a very economical way to add custom elements. Kelli Crowe stitched the
cake design as well as the title and a border around her page with embroidery
floss and a needle.

SOURCES Pen: EK Success (black), American Crafts (white). Floss: DMC. Design: Kelli Crowe.

Fill in
stitched designs
with paint, chalk, or
colored pencils.

What you'll need: a pencil • cardstock • a foam or rubber pad • a paper piercer • a needle and thread

1 Lightly trace or draw your
design with a pencil. If you're
not comfortable with your
drawing skills, trace a clip-art
image or font.

2 Place the cardstock on the
foam mat and use the piercing
tool to punch holes along
the lines.

3 Stitch along your design, using
a backstitch. When you're
finished, erase any stray pencil
marks that still show.

stamp a background

Customize your layout by stamping designs on the background paper. Lisa Russo stamped a subtle pattern on green cardstock in watermark ink. Watermark inks create an image slightly darker than the background paper. She also stamped the design on the white paper borders, using several ink colors. Once she'd stamped the design, she cut the sheet into wavy strips to bookend her layout.

SOURCES Font: Serafina BT off the Internet. Rubber stamps: Hero Arts. Ink: Tsukineko. Acrylic paint: Li'l Davis Designs. Chipboard letters: Advantus. Brads: American Crafts. Pearls: Westrim Crafts. Design: Lisa Russo.

When stamping rows, use the ends of the stamp as a guide to keep rows straight, or draw pencil lines and erase later.

What you'll need: color ink pads • rubber stamps • cardstock

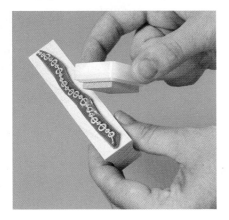

1 Press the stamp into the ink pad until the entire image is coated or, if you're using a small ink pad, press the pad to the stamp.

2 Apply the stamp to the page using even pressure. Avoid rocking as you may end up with stray ink marks. Alternate ink colors and patterns to create different looks.

make it tonight

SHORT ON SCRAPBOOKING TIME? Try adapting this creative design that can be made in no time at all.

I have known you since you were a child - practically your entire life. I have watched you grow and become a beautiful young woman, now a mother, who is watching her own children grow.

Jennifer & Jackson
May 3, 2008

Grow
design by Kelly Goree

MATERIALS
photo: one horizontal 7×4⅞"
cardstock: light blue, white
paper: two patterns
other: chipboard accents; ink; button

Trim a 2×12" strip of patterned paper, ink the edges, and adhere it 1½" from the left-hand side of a 12×12" piece of cardstock. Format your journaling on a curve and print it on a 7×4½" piece of white cardstock. Trim the cardstock to match the curve of the text, then add it next to the striped paper as shown. Curve the right-hand side of the photo, ink the edges, and adhere it below the white cardstock. Curve the right-hand side of a 7×2⅝" patterned-paper piece and place it below the photo. Cover the curve with a chipboard flower and add a chipboard title. Kelly swapped a flower in place of the "o," accenting it with a button.

 SOURCES Cardstock: Bazzill Basics Paper. Patterned paper, chipboard accents, button: BasicGrey. Font: Rockwell off the Internet. Ink: ColorBox by Clearsnap.

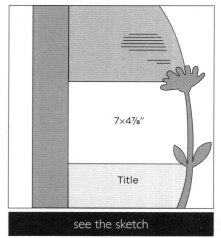

7×4⅞"

Title

see the sketch